Cathy's Book

A frozen Memory in time.

If found call
(650) 266-8233

Stewart / Weisman / Brigg

AN Age Still to Live.

RUNNING PRESS
PHILADELPHIA · LONDON

V = ♥ = ?

42 Entertainment™

Cathy

Library of Congress Control Number: 2006901472
ISBN-13: 978-0-7624-2656-0
ISBN-10: 0-7624-2656-X

was here!

→ Sky Ber

Cover design by Alicia Freile
Interior design by Cathy Briggs
Edited by Andra Serlin

Emma thought the
good folks at CoverGirl
and BeingGirl.com would
kick-start my career and
help me get the message
out. She was right, I was
wrong, what else is new?
Thanks, guys.

HISTORY
SUX

Sky Girl

RUNNING PRESS BOOK PUBLISHERS
125 SOUTH TWENTY-SECOND STREET
PHILADELPHIA, PENNSYLVANIA 19103-4399

www.runningpress.com

ROCK

LOST

9 8 7 6 5 4 3 2

Digit on the right indicates the number of this printing

Jan 30, Afternoon
(Hour of the Monkey)

- Dumped by boyfriend last night.
- Horrendous fight with Mom this morning.
- Forgot about math test this afternoon.

<screen goes wavy—cue FLASHBACK sound f/x for scene from our heroine's morning, orning, rning…>

Mom came in from her graveyard shift while I was getting ready for school. I was scratching this little itchy, sore spot inside my elbow, when all of a sudden Mom grabbed my wrist so hard with her strong nurse hands that her knuckles turned white. "What is this?"

"You're hurting me!"

She tapped the itchy spot. "You think I don't know a needle-track? You think I'm that stupid?"

"Oh, great. Now you think I'm shooting drugs." It was so unfair. "Have you been drinking again? Do you know me at all?"

The contempt in her eyes was like a slap. "I suppose you're going to say you got a shot from the school nurse? I can call her, Cathy. Think fast. Pick the right lie."

"Screw you!" I yelled, and I slammed out the front door.

She stood on the porch and yelled, so the whole world could hear. "I see kids just like you in the ER every night. You want to flunk out of school? Be an artist? Here's a bulletin from the real world, Cathy. You know who bought this house? I did. Your Dad got to lie around in his bathrobe all day painting because I made the money. So if you want to flunk out, hey, fine, be my guest. I just hope your latest boyfriend can keep you in style after you graduate, 'cause I sure won't."

—> Should have said, "No fear there, Mom—the boyfriend just dumped me." **</flashback>**

It was a "cut your ear off" kind of a day!!

✂—————————————— cut along dotted line.

Now it's after school. Mom's still sleeping. I'll head over to Emma's in a sec. We're supposed to work on this big research paper for Biology, but the truth is, I just don't want to be in the house when Mom wakes up. ~~It's not like she really gives a damn about me anymore. She just doesn't want more hassle in her life.~~

I'm never going to let myself get that bitter. Never, never, never.

But what about my arm?

There's a little bruise, just inside my left elbow, with a tiny dot in the middle. It **does** look like a needle-mark, actually, only I haven't used any. Must have been a mosquito or a spider-bite or something.

—Just heard Mom's alarm go off. Spidey-sense tingling. Time to get out.

Jan 30, Evening
(Hour of the Rat. Listen for faint sound of sharp teeth in the dark.) *Over At Emma's Place*

First sound I heard after letting myself into Emma's apartment: her fingers drumming away on her keyboard. Funny, familiar sound: soothing as rain pattering on a window. Coming into her bedroom, I tried to find a place to sit on her bed, which was quilted w/ approximately 1 Zillion index cards w/ notes for our essay—each topic written up in a different color of ink.

I felt the first rush of a Science Contact High, so I took out my sketch pad in self- defense and started doodling. I had just managed to sell my first cartoons to an online site. The money wasn't much, but it was a rush to be a Real Artist who got Paid for Work, and I was desperate to do more. Plus it beat trying to follow Emma into the Science Zone... "So, where's your dad today?"

"Tai Pei, I think. Or maybe Shenzen. He's coming back for Valentine's Day."

*

Emma turned around and put on her Lecturing Nun face, left over from way too many years at the Maryknoll Convent School in Hong Kong. "Did you *know*, Miss Vickers, that many *bats* have lifespans 3 to 4 times as long as we might expect for mammals of their size? Researchers *believe* they have a gene which produces free-radical scrubbing enzymes, which retard

the height of boredom.

2.

cellular oxidation. Some also show increased telomerase production, and—"
She looked narrowly at me. "You do have notes for our paper, right? You
promised you would bring notes."

I pretended not to hear her, deeply absorbed in doodle of a little bat with
Emma's small round Chinese face and small round English glasses.

"Cathy! This is due in three days! You promised me I wouldn't end up
doing the whole thing by myself."

"Let's write about poisons instead," I suggested. "Curare. Strychnine.
Arsenic. Poisons that make your tongue swell until it blocks your throat.
Poisons that make blood run out of your eyes and give you anthrax."

"Anthrax isn't a poison, it's—"

"One that you could sprinkle in someone's hot chocolate and then watch
all the blood vessels in his face burst so it turns into a little red sprinkler—"

"I guess this is still about Victor," she said dryly. "Why not think positive?
Maybe he had a really good reason for dumping you."

I gave her a look. Emma never especially liked Victor, possibly because
the first time she met him she threw up all over the back of his airplane.
She hates being embarrassed. Still, she could at least have pretended to be
sympathetic.

"For instance," she said brightly, "he worked at a biotech company, right?
So maybe he found a hair you shed on his coat and sequenced it in the lab
and compared it to his own DNA and discovered that if you ever did get
married, you were doomed to give birth to baby weasels."

"I hate you," I said.

"I know."

*

I told Emma about the fight with my mom, and showed her the bruise.
"You can see why she thought it was a needle mark," she said.

A deep feeling of unease began to creep over me. "Emma, listen. A
few days ago Victor took me to this crazy place called the Musée Mécanique,
down on Pier 45. We stayed there until they closed up, and then Victor
gave me a ride home. He came over to our house, and we stayed up
really late talking. Lights low. Soft music…. You know that moment,

google—▷ website(!!!)

when you and a guy both realize you're about to kiss?"

"Sure," Emma said bravely.

[(Yeah, sure, right....)] — *um, no offense right?...*

"He reached over me to turn the music down, and that moment happened. It seemed to take forever. His mouth was over mine so long my lips started to tingle. And then he croaked, 'How about some hot chocolate?'"

Emma blinked. "Maybe he's not into girls?"

"I don't know why he stopped! Anyway, he makes this really strong hot chocolate, and we talk some more."

"More talking?"

"Shut up." I gave her a friendly finger gesture. "I'm waiting to get back to the kissing vibe, only now I'm *so sleepy*."

"It was really late," Emma said.

"No, I mean like, sleepier than that. So I decided to take things into my own hands, you know. I hauled myself up, and I put a hand on his neck, and I leaned towards him…"

"*And???*"

"I fell off the couch."

"You *what!*"

I started to flush. "I fell off the couch. Stop laughing, you cow!" I took the pillow off Emma's bed and belted her with it. "I couldn't make my muscles do anything. It was like the time I went to the dentist and had three valiums by accident."

"That was hilarious," Emma said absently, but her smile slowly faded. Carefully she said, "Did you have your clothes on when you woke up?"

"Yeah. It's not like he needs to drug me to get…"—I felt my face coloring—"*Whatever*, you know. He could just ask. I'm sure he knows that. Only he never asked. Anyway, here's the weird thing: when I woke up the next day, I was still dressed, but I was upstairs in my bed. I tried to get up a couple of times in the morning, but I felt so stoned I just *couldn't*. It wasn't until Mom's alarm went off at four in the afternoon that I could force myself to get up and pretend I'd been at school all day."

Worry made little lines around Emma's eyes and mouth. "You think

Victor *drugged* you?"

"It doesn't make any sense. But..." I tapped the bruise inside my elbow. "This was hurting when I woke up."

She blinked. "Your arm?" I nodded. "And two days later he calls up and says he doesn't want to see you anymore?"

"Right."

Emma swirled around in her Science Officer Command Chair, thoughtfully kicking her feet. "Look, I like a good conspiracy as much as the next girl, but if you woke up with your clothes on and no signs of, um, extra activities, Victor probably wasn't slipping you a mickey. The mark on your arm is probably a spider-bite. And as for him dumping you..."

"He's too old to be wasting time with me anyway," I recited, to save her the bother. I tried to hit Emma with the pillow again, but she blocked with her feet.

"Didn't you tell me Victor was getting calls from this woman he worked with—"

"Carla. Carla Beckman."

"Right," Emma said. "So probably Victor just decided to go out with, you know, a grown-up."

"Gee, thanks."

"Here to soothe," she said. "Can we work on our essay now?"

Jan 30, Evening, Even Later, Dammit.
(Hour of the Ox)

The Hour of the Ox is between 1 and 3 AM. It's called *Ch'ou* in Chinese. So says this book Victor got me in Chinatown, the ***T'ung Shu***, which is like a Chinese Old Farmers Almanac for Very Weird Farmers.

*

I'm back from Emma's place. Mom's at work. House is

empty

empty

empty

So empty it makes my ears ring.

*

5.

Sharpest memory of Dad: him padding around in his bathrobe every morning, cooking French toast or pancakes. Most days I never even saw him eat; he was always busy behind the counter, serving us first because

A) Mom was exhausted from the end of her shift, and

B) I was late for school.

Now I wish we'd made him sit down with us more often.

*

Found Mom's supply of Gordon's and made myself a Gin & Tonic, which is what she does when she can't sleep. This is what breakfast looks like, since Dad died: me eating Frosted Flakes and Mom making a G & T so she can get to sleep in the daytime.

So far the gin doesn't seem to be doing much for me. I keep walking and walking around the house, like a wind-up toy that never winds down.

*

Fortune Telling by Physical Sensation

"Ringing in the ears in the Hour of Ch'ou: You will quarrel with a loved one."

*

Still not sleepy. Going to make another G&T. Think I probably put too much tonic in the first one.

Oh, God, it's late. I should be working on this biology paper. Do it for the team, Cathy! This isn't about your own selfish need for sleep—we have a higher goal here! Maintaining Emma's 4.0!!!!!

<groan>

Must remember to set alarm clock when I get back to room.

zzZzZzzzzzZZzzzzzzzzZZzZzZzzzz....

Jan 30 Eve— oops. Jan 31, I mean.
Call it Jan 30+, approximately O'Dark Thirty in the Morning (Hour of the Gin and Tonic)

Just re-re-read entry for day I met V, creepy worthless lying creepy JERK. I sniveled continuously, no doubt dribbling snot into 4th G&T.

DON'T SEE WHY HE COULDN'T JUST TELL ME WHAT I WAS DOING WRONG, FOR GOD'S SAKE!!!!!!!!

6.

November 11, Morning. Veterans Day

Holiday Monday, so no school. Everybody else either working or spending the day w/ family. Even Emma's dad in town for weekend.

Mom still working graveyard shift. House empty and depressing. Looking through my window outside I can see wet leaves on the sidewalk, November trees going bare. Things are always dying on Veterans Day.

If this were a war year, if this were 1918 or 1944, I wouldn't be the only girl whose dad was never coming home. Think of that: a whole generation of us, daughters or young wives, waiting for a car that will never roll into the driveway. Waiting for a door that will never open again.

*

November 11, EVENING

Met the strangest guy today. Sort of a jerk, but an interesting jerk. Not sure how I should feel. Not sure how I do feel.

*

Decided to catch a bus into the City & Golden Gate Park. Took my sketchbook down on the seawall. Partly cloudy, partly foggy—light the color of salt glinting over the ocean. Rocks slimy with seaweed, mottled fans and strings of it. White rush of surf, smack of it dropping onto the shingle.

10 yards out, a black cormorant was standing on a boulder. He had his wings stretched wide, wide. Our eyes met. That shouldn't happen with a bird, but it did. His were yellow: ancient: inhuman.

Victor

"You got the wings wrong."

I looked up. Good-looking jerk leaning over my shoulder, scoping out my sketch. "Get lost." I said. *very ladylike!*

"Head's okay, I guess."

"Glad you approve. Get lost."

7.

☆ ARTGIRL ☆

MISSION:
Sketch with great passion.
Develop technique and
Enlarge Soul!

TARGET:
Golden Gate Park

man's bottle green,
vintage, silk shirt,
unbuttoned & untucked,
as if by accident.
(No such thing as accident
with us. See Artgirl
with tousled just-woke-
up hair, bet your bottom
dollar she spent 20 mins
in the mirror to get the
exact perfect tousle!
This is what it means
to be Artgirl!!

black leather
jacket

black T

black
pants

mid-calf
boots
(to go with
jacket)

GEAR
① 1x attaché case,
filched from Mom's
supply: russet colored
leather, soft sided
— classy!

② 1x classic matte black
sketch book.

③ Faber-Castell PITT
charcoals

④ Koh-I-Noor inks

⑤ 2 pens and 2 brushes

⑥ steel wool, Krylon fixative
(one good jostle on BarT
can smudge 2 hrs of work)

8.

"Victor Chan," he said. He stuck out his hand.

Confession time: he was a really, really good-looking guy. Early twenties, maybe, half-Asian, with a fascinating face: pale skin, black hair, unexpected eyes: dark green, like wet jade. I imagined a Chinese father and the mother a Scot, red-haired and hot tempered. I appreciate guy's bodies more than most girls. I look at them. The history of art is a thousand years of nude studies, after all: I like the weight and shift of muscles moving under skin. Two accessories with a bit of style: a jade pendant that he wore around his neck, and a nice old pocket watch that hung from his belt loop on a short steel chain.

I pegged him as the kind of jock that has a thing for smart girls. You see these guys, second-stringers on the football team; they stand around the edges of the Jock Huddle listening to raunchy talk about cheerleaders, but they fall for the smart girl with library eyes. I wear the Smart Girl colors (Edgy Division)—black outfits or vintage clothes, sketch pad, glasses with interesting frames—so I get these hits every now and then.

I shook his hand. "Nice to meet you, Victor Chan. Go away."

"A real artist has to know how to take criticism," he said.

"I'm not a real artist. I'm just a sulky wannabe." I smiled and gave him a well-known finger gesture. "Bye-bye, Victor Chan."

He laughed and bent down beside my shoulder, studying my sketch, a little closer than necessary. I meant to tell him to get lost, meaning it: but in the pale slant light of the afternoon I got distracted by the exact fall of the fine hairs along his forearm. Time slowed down, then: opened up: stretching the pause between one wave breaking …

…and the next.

I had the strangest feeling the cormorant was holding time open for me. Pushing it back with his wings.

Dare

"It's a good drawing, but the wings are too big."

I said, "I got his mouth the right size."

He grinned. "Draw me."

"I don't think so."

10.

"Scared?"

"Better things to do with my time."

"Drawing birds?"

"For example."

Stalemate.

I have a good Scornful Stare ™—cold, distant, belittling. I know it's good because I practice it in the mirror. I tried it on him.

He laughed. "Draw me. I'll pay you what the picture's worth."

"I don't want to." I felt out of my element. He must have been only four or five years older than the guys at my high school, but it felt like a big difference. "Hey, jerk. No Means No." I stuffed my sketch book into my leather case. Stood up and checked my pockets for bus fare.

The cormorant shook his head at me, displeased. He flapped his wings once, twice, and paddled his feet irritably up and down.

"Okay, so you're not ready," Victor said. "Keep writing only in your diary and showing your pictures only to your best friend, then."

"Screw you!" I glared at him. "How much will you pay for that drawing?"

"Depends on what it's worth."

I pulled the sketch book back out of my case and grabbed a pen. "Sit up on the wall there."

He grinned. "Oh, I see. You're one of those girls that needs to get mad before she—"

"Shut up!"

He shut up.

I drew.

#

Portrait

I drew him as he would look at age sixty, imagining the droop at the corners of his mouth and the hollowing under the cheeks. He'd go lean, not fat, I thought. Pouches under the eyes, flat bone showing under thin skin at the temples. The smooth skin around his eyes creased up and leathery. A liver-spot or two.

I almost always draw people a different age than they actually are. It's like a compulsion. Some people are shocked when they see my portraits. They think I'm just trying to be a witch. I'm not. Well, mostly not. Anyone can do a likeness. That's in the hand. Art should be in the eye, too. In the heart.

When I finished, he looked at the drawing for a long time. I figured he'd hate it and I wouldn't get any money, but that was okay.

"Getting a little revenge?" he said at last.

"Don't flatter yourself. This is what I do. I imagine how people are going to look. Fast-forward them. Here are my friends." I flipped over the sketch book, showing a few others—me and Emma at 28 and 40 and 60 and 75. Mom at 90, withered up in a nursing home bed.

He gave me a curious look. "Do people like it when you draw them like this?"

"They hate it."

"I bet." He turned away for a moment, looking out over the sea. "It's a funny thing, watching people get old. ...You know what they call this day in Canada? It's not Veterans Day there. It's Remembrance Day. It's a big deal there, bigger than Memorial Day here. They lost so many men, you know, at Ypres, and Verdun. Eight hundred thousand men killed at the Somme. Flanders, and god-forsaken Vimy Ridge. 'In Flanders Fields the poppies grow...' Everyone wears poppies." He trailed off.

I tried to think of something to say, so I wouldn't look dumb for not being up on the First World War. "There's this painting by Chagall called *Cemetery Gates*," I said. He did it during the war. No soldiers, no battles, it's really very peaceful and beautiful, in a way, but you can feel the weight of the war in every brushstroke. Like a, a requiem." The guy was looking at me, very serious now. I felt awkward. "My dad was a painter. He used to quiz me on pictures—date and artist, you know. *The Night Watch*, Rembrandt, 1642. *Las Meninas*, Velazquez, 1656. *Cemetery Gates*, Chagall, 1917. It sounds stupid, but I guess that's really the way I know history. World War One is *Cemetery Gates* and Otto Dix's *Self-Portrait as a Soldier*. World War Two is *Guernica*... Do you know Chagall?"

"No."

"Oh," I said, feeling stupid.

He regarded me. "You're an interesting girl." I kept my mouth shut. "I have this...friend," he said, stumbling over the word. "It's her fifty-seventh birthday today. Makes you think," he said.

"Remembrance Day," I said.

He smiled. "Yeah."

"My name's Cathy," I said. I tore Victor's portrait out of the sketch book. "So what's it worth to you?"

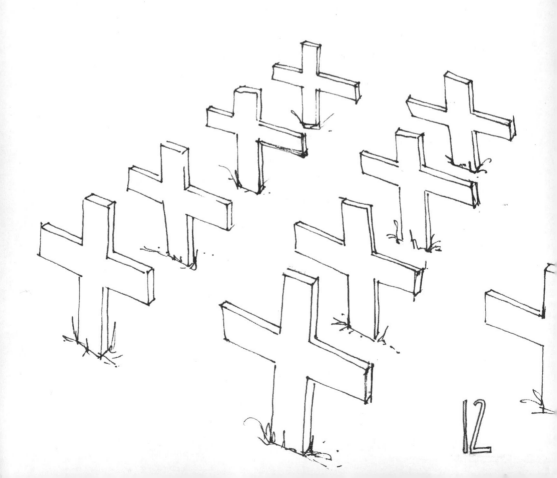

12

13.

Jerk.

New theory about my arm.

VICTOR IS A VAMPIRE!!!!! Can just see that creep squatting over me on my VERY OWN COUCH and SUCKING OUT MY BLOOD with a TINY CONCEALED FANG in his TONGUE!!!!!

Oh, gross.

I think I'm going to throw up.

Jan 30++, 3:17 AM
(Hour of the Late Night DJ)

Washed mouth out with Scope. Feel much better now. Clear-headed. Have regained perspective. No longer interested in V. Not jealous type. DO wonder what is wrong with *him*!

Jan 30+++, So Late At Night It's Early
(Hour of the Street Cleaner)

Our First Date

Victor took me flying in his Uncle's private plane. I'm not making this up. He said my picture made him see the world differently, and he wanted to do the same for me.

Emma hated the idea of being trapped in a little plane, but I made her come along anyway to make sure the Big Bad College Boy didn't try any funny stuff.

Air feels *slippery* at 4000 feet. With no road or sidewalk, it feels like you're just about to slide off the sky.   But it was beautiful, and exciting—> fields, hills, sea checkerboarding under us.

#

So we're up in Victor's plane, Emma turning green in the seat behind me. The first time we turned, my shoulder thumped into the door. I found myself looking at the ground through my window and I sort of squeaked.

He was funny and kind and his bomber jacket had all these tough, exciting smells: leather and machine oil and cold mornings.

Q: "When did you learn to fly?"

A: "Junior High Shop class was full, so I took Pilot's License instead." Wiseass.

He asked if I had a job and I said I was a student and he said, Berkeley? And I said, *mumble mumble,* even though I could hear Emma's eyes rolling behind me, because I didn't want him to think I was just another high school kid.

Then we hit some turbulence and Emma found out there weren't any airsickness bags in the plane.

*

Five Most Amazing Things About Victor

5   Our first evening date, he took me out to a Cambodian restaurant called Angkor Wat. *Cambodian?!?* We split a Banana Blossom Salad and a creamy chicken curry with lemon grass that came in a coconut shell, with sweet Cambodian coffee afterwards. Victor paid for it all in cash. My last date with GrungeGuy was Dutch treat at Burger King. Of course I would NEVER say a BF *has* to be funny and sophisticated and take you nice places and pay for it afterwards. But he should *try*.

4   Victor knows how to cheat at cards. Says he grew up in Nevada, where they put a pack of cards in every baby's crib. I made him teach me how to use a Mechanic's Grip to deal off the bottom of the deck, but he made me promise first that I must Use The Art Only For Good and Never For Evil.

3   His hands, strong wrists, quick brown fingers, bending back a pack of cards for a waterfall shuffle. Omigod.

2   He knows not one word of Chinese, but he is fluent in *French*. I only found this out because one day we were out

14.

together and his cell phone rang and suddenly he was gabbling away *En Francais,* laughing and making jokes. I asked why on earth he had picked up French. He said, "I spent some time with this bunch of French guys in Algeria and their English sucked, so I figured I better learn."

… and the #1 most amazing thing about Victor Chan…

<drumroll>

1   He laughs at my jokes.

*

I wish he hadn't dumped me. I wish Dad hadn't died. I wish Mom and I didn't fight all the time.

God, I'm tired.

Jan 31, —Meaning, the Morning After the Night Before —(Hour of the Splitting Headache)

Forgot to set the freaking alarm!!!!!!!!!!!!!!

Woke up to the sound of my answering machine getting the phone. Emma's voice blaring irritably through the speaker. "Cathy? Cathy? Are you there? I know you're there." I thought about crawling out of bed, but someone had turned up the gravity and it seemed too far. "Okay, then, be that way," Emma said. "Just *don't go to his house, and don't set anything on fire!*"

<Click.>

'Don't go to his house'— How offensive! Like my best friend thinks I would hang around and *beg*? As for that fire-setting crack, that was almost three years ago, it was a really old cheap car, and I think I have my temper under a lot better control.

Besides, that was Jenny's older brother Brad, and he *so* deserved it.

*

Took a long shower to clear my head. Feel better now.

Checked e-mail. One message from Emma: "Don't go to his house!"

Jeez. As if.

Jan 31, Evening
(In Which a Bear of Very Little Brain Goes To
Victor's House and Finds a Very Curyus Messaj)

I'm not the jealous type. I just don't like being jerked around.

All I was going to do was show up on his doorstep and ask what the hell was up. It wasn't like I wanted another date. I wouldn't take him back if he came CRAWLING ON HIS HANDS AND KNEES.

After school I took BART into the city and then a bus to Haight-Ashbury. My ArtGirl costume was OK camouflage for mingling with the Haight's tat-and-piercing crowd. I was wearing my Guess What You're Missing outfit: fitted black leather jacket, low-rider jeans and boots that went Stomp, Stomp, Stomp up the hill to Victor's Uncle's house.

Victor had brought me by this place once, when he had to pick up some keys, but he said he wasn't supposed to have visitors, so I had never actually been inside. Victor didn't say it directly, but I got the feeling his Uncle was kind of traditional, and didn't approve of Victor slumming with Western girls. I figured the Uncle was another Astronaut, like Emma's dad—HK Chinese, with a residence in the States, but spending most of his time in Asia. I'd never actually met him, but obviously he was loaded. There was the plane, of course, and this gorgeous place, a two-and-a-half story Victorian House on the Hill right next to Golden Gate Park. That's probably a five million dollar house.

My thighs were burning by the time I got to the top of the block. The property hid behind a high wall, backed by a bamboo hedge and pierced by a single arch. I leaned into the curve of the gate for a second, gathering my courage and my breath.

My eye fell on the mailbox.

Of course, it would be wrong to pry into Victor's mail. Obviously. But there couldn't be any harm in just carrying it—unopened of course— up the steep path to the front door, could there? That would be positively *helpful*, right?

I reached into the mailbox casually, as if I did this every day. Anyone watching would have thought it perfectly natural, as long as they couldn't hear

16

my heartbeat rattling like a runaway train. Stupid guilty heartbeat.

I don't know what I was expecting—A Valentine from the odious Carla From the Lab, maybe?—but there was nothing hand-addressed, just standard computer-printed letters to Victor Chan: a LensCrafters Savings Alert, two credit card come-ons, and a property tax notice, along with grocery circulars and a thin magazine called *Science News*. Nothing exciting.

—Wait a sec. *Property tax notice?*

I stuffed everything back in the mailbox, took my cell phone out of my purse, and called Emma. "You weren't in school today," she complained. "We were supposed to work on the Biology paper. I know you say you can't get interested in school any more, but jeez, Cathy—just hold it together six more months and you can at least get your GED. Besides, it's my mark, too."

"Gosh, wouldn't want to bring you down to a 3.95," I said impatiently. "Listen, remember how Victor has this rich uncle?"

"With the plane?"

"And the house—Victor was house-sitting for him."

"Okay."

"Do you think the IRS would send property tax notices to a house-sitter, or the legal owner?"

"Owner, obviously."

"That's what I thought, too. Thanks Em."

"Cathy, wait," Emma said suspiciously. "Why are you asking this? Where are you?"

"Gotta go," I said. "Catch you later."

"You aren't at his *house*, are you? You aren't looking through his *mail?*"

"My lawyers advise me to take the 5th. Look, he lied to us. This is *Victor's house.*"

"Cathy! Maybe it's in his name as a legal convenience. The Uncle spends most of his time in Asia. Dad pays my apartment bills, but lots of them come addressed to me."

"From the IRS?" Silence. "I've never seen the famous Uncle, Em. *What if he doesn't exist?* What if it really does belong to Victor—the house, the plane, everything?"

Emma snorted. "How would a twenty-three year old guy get that kind of money?"

"Yeah," I said. "That's just what I'm asking myself."

"Oh," Emma said. And then, slowly, "*Oh*."

"Could have inherited it," I said.

"Patent," Emma said. "Software. Bio-tech. This is Silicon Valley, after all. Or he could be a pop-star or something."

"Right. Sure."

"But that's not what you're thinking, is it?"

"No," I admitted. Victor had never talked about computers—or being a rock star, for that matter. According to him, he was just another lab tech at Intrepid Biotech—$15/hour sequencing DNA from fruit flies or something.

"You're thinking about drugs," Emma said.

"Yeah."

"You're thinking he's young and rich and he has a private plane, and that means he's smuggling drugs."

"Yeah."

I could practically hear the whir of Emma's brain spinning over the phone. "Or you're thinking he's young, he's rich, *he works in a lab and he does a lot of overtime*," she said. "So maybe he's not smuggling drugs … maybe he's making them? XTC. Rohypnol. Or designer stuff. He stumbled across something in the lab, some freaky Human Growth Hormone high or Fetal Tissue Extract Elixir of Life. That's what you're thinking."

"It is now."

"Jesus," Emma said.

"Yeah," I said. I looked up at the tall bamboo hedge that walled off Victor's property from the rest of the world. "If he has the job he says he does, he shouldn't be making enough to afford a cardboard box in San Francisco, let alone this place."

"Cathy, you get away from that house," Emma said. "You get on the bus and come straight home."

"What? I can't hear you. Terrible reception."

"*Cathy!*"

18.

"Oops—you're breaking up," I said brightly.

"Don't go in, and don't set anything on fi—"

"Bye!" I flipped the cell phone shut, stuck the tax notice back in the mailbox, and walked briskly through the gate before I could chicken out.

Jan 31ˢᵗ, Evening
(Hour of the Hunted Felon)

Ninety minutes of typing and I'm still wired like I was mainlining espresso.

Not sure what to do yet. Sensible part of me says, pretend none of this ever happened. Less sensible part would like to find V and deliver swift kick to family jewels.

The good news is, I don't turn 18 for another week, so if the cops burst in, I'll probably get tried as a minor.

OK. That thought wasn't as soothing as I had hoped. More typing....

Three Old Men

It was twilight, that time when the blue overhead is deepening fast, and shadows are thickening down on the ground. The path beyond the gate was marked with white pebbles, a dim pale track winding uphill through what felt like a miniature mountainside. It was weirdly quiet. None of the clanking buzz of San Francisco made it over the hedge—no cars honking their horns or crazy homeless people or deathwish bicycle couriers. I could hear the ragged sound of my own breath, and feel the thump of my heart. Thickets of bamboo rustled and whispered to one another as I climbed past.

Halfway up the hill to the house, the path skirted a dell that had been cut into the slope to hold a small pond, its still water midnight blue in the deepening dusk. On the far bank, a mossy boulder, a gnarled pine tree, and a white crane stood in a group, with their reflections dimly mirrored in the dark water. The marble boulder was white and spidered with thin blue lines, like veins running under an old man's skin. The pine's roots were knobby and knuckled as arthritic fingers. The crane turned his slow white head and regarded me with one cold yellow eye. I had the strongest feeling that a moment before they had been talking together, three old men discussing serious business, suddenly interrupted when I blundered into their private conversation.

19.

"Sorry!" I muttered. The crane watched me come on for some steps, obviously displeased. Finally he beat his wings and climbed heavily into the air. The top of the path was dominated by an ancient plum tree, already flowering in the cold spring air. The crane flapped heavily into its branches and settled there, half-hidden in the cloud of blossoms, glaring at me.

On the Porch

The crane was still watching when I got to the house porch. It was nearly six o'clock, and I wasn't sure if Victor would be home. I had to admit I was having second thoughts about this whole idea. Wanting to kick the butt of a boyfriend who dumps you for no reason is natural and just. It's a little different to get in the face of a really successful drug dealer.

On the other hand, I have a slight flaw in my character that makes it hard for me to suffer in silence. I rang the doorbell. Nobody came. I tried the knob. It was unlocked. I turned it and cracked the door. "Victor!" No answer. But he wouldn't have left the door unlocked if he were going out, surely? He must be inside, *pretending* not to have heard me. "Victor, answer the door!" Still no response.

I swore and stomped up and down the porch a couple of times. Golden Gate Park stretched out below me, hilly and green and dim. Further out, over the ocean, the last afterglow of sunset burned in the crack between the sea and the sky. The crane in the plum tree was still watching me. "I guess I'd better go," I said. He opened his beak as if yawning. "I didn't ask your opinion." He clacked his long yellow bill at me dismissively. "Yeah?" I said. "Well, screw you."

I turned my back on him and marched inside.

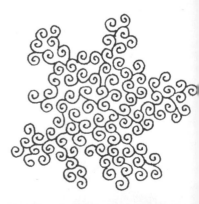

February 1st, Just past midnight.
Still typing, typing, typing....

I know, I know: I shouldn't have gone in. Let the chick without sin cast the first stone.

Oops—just looked at the clock. Good grief. Nearly done here—just a few more minutes, and then I really will get to work on that Biology paper....

The House

The door opened into a little entryway with rooms on either side, and a passage leading to the kitchen. "Victor?"

No answer, but I thought I heard a squeak, like a door opening on the other side of the house. I tip-toed forward, feeling intensely curious and rather guilty, too. It reminded me of babysitting when I was thirteen and fourteen, poking into the parents' bedroom after the kids were asleep. I got over that phase in a hurry after I found a stack of magazines in the Millers' bedroom that I would rather not have seen.

Victor's kitchen was beautiful. He had a gorgeous restaurant-caliber range on an island in the middle, a big butcher-block table for food preparation, double sinks, mesh bags of garlic and red onions and dried peppers hanging from hooks in the ceiling overhead. There was a wine-rack too in one corner, with forty or fifty bottles in it. I pulled one out at random. The label was in French. I didn't recognize the brand name—Chateau Petrus—but the year on the bottle was 1945.

There was a door at the back of the kitchen. When I pushed it open it made the squeak I'd heard in the foyer. Victor must have slipped out the back way when I came in the front. I ran back to the front porch. The crane was beating heavily up out of the plum tree, as if disturbed. Footsteps went crunching down the gravel path. "Get back here, you gutless wonder!" I yelled, but the footsteps hurried away into the gloom, soon muffled by distance and thickets of bamboo.

Fine, then. If that's the way he wanted to play it.... I turned back into Victor's house, this time without a tremor of guilt. If he didn't have the guts to talk to me, he deserved what he got, didn't he?

Cemetery Gates

I went back to the kitchen and opened the fridge. If I wasn't going to get my apology from Victor, he could at least give me a snack. I found a Ghirardelli chocolate bar in the refrigerator door—perfect. Munching triumphantly on that, I poked my nose through doors until I found a study—bookshelves and paintings, and Victor's fancy ultra-thin lap-top sitting on a beautiful antique mahogany desk that made the computer seem garish and out of place. The desk was littered with papers, and what looked like money too. Odd, that. It wasn't like Victor to be messy.

I took a curious step forward and then stopped dead in my tracks. Hanging above the desk was a painting by Chagall—*Cemetery Gates*.

When I mentioned it, Victor said he'd never heard of Chagall. But here it was, hanging in his study. I leaned forward until my nose was nearly touching it. Certainly not a print; I could see the weave of the canvas under the oil paints. Either it was a heck of a forgery or the real thing. I had the creepy feeling it was the real thing.

Goosebumps prickled along my arms and down my back. Either:

    a)   Victor had lied two months ago when he said he didn't know the piece, or

    b)   He had gone out and bought a genuine Chagall after I mentioned it.

Underneath the Chagall, in a simple frame sitting beside the lap-top, was the portrait of Victor I had sketched on the first day we met.

My heart was pounding and my face was flushed. What did it mean? My picture, framed and standing under a genuine Chagall…. What was he thinking? How could those things mean so much to him—when he didn't even want to see me anymore?

(Feb 1, Late at night, in the middle of typing…)

Just went and looked up auction prices on Chagall on the Web. Cemetery Gates was listed as being in a "private collection." A random Chagall painting of a bunch of flowers in a vase, not nearly as good, had recently been auctioned for $610,000.00

    Oh, my god.

22.

The Desk

The rest of the desk was messy—not at all like Victor. All the drawers were pulled out and open, and there were papers scattered everywhere: a couple of old passports, various legal documents and licenses, and a bunch of colorful money from other countries—France and Spain, Morocco, Algeria, Viet Nam, and Cambodia. There were a few handwritten letters, too—probably from a grandmother. (Who else writes letters by hand anymore?)

Curiouser and curiouser.

Sticking out from under the letter was a little black day-timer Victor often carried with him. I riffled guiltily through it, looking for my name, and found the vile Carla's instead—they'd met three times last week, including going for lunch a few hours before Victor took me to the Musée Mécanique and then served me some of his Curiously Strong Hot Chocolate.

I felt my throat cramp up. Served me right for spying. I looked away from the desk for a moment, up at the luminous blues and grays of *Cemetery Gates*. That archway between this world and wherever my dad had gone.

To hell with Victor anyway, I said to an imaginary Carla. He's a lying creep who's hiding something big and nasty. You're welcome to him, sister.

I flipped through the day-timer to the current date.

Notice how much less crazy I was then? Didn't even think of dialing the #...

Jan 31

5-6 *** New Chair ***

The entry was starred and circled in red. Obviously a big deal, though it seemed like a lot of excitement over a piece of furniture. The last entry in pen was an appointment for the next night—

Feb 1

7 pm   Eight Ancestors

The desk drawers were all open. The bottom was loose on one, and a slim pouch had started to slip through. I picked it up. It was an old leather case, worn and soft, about the size of a paperback book; the sort of thing you might put money in when you were traveling, or a passport, to keep it hidden underneath your shirt or tucked inside the waistband of your pants. I opened the end of the pouch and shook it.

I guess I was expecting a drug-runner's get-away kit: fake ID, a handful

23

of $100 dollar bills, a Colombian passport and an account number for a Swiss bank. Instead what I found were more puzzling, personal treasures. Old letters, and a family tree. A wedding invitation in French. A stack of old newspaper clippings. A family photograph: a pretty young brunette holding a girl of two or two and a half, dressed in a ridiculously poofy white dress, all lace and white stockings. Dad stood behind with his arm around Mom's waist, looking on and smiling.

The dad was Victor.

I stared in shock, leaning closer. There was no doubt about it. Unless he had a twin brother, the man in the picture was Victor. The young wife was Western, fine-featured, with a laughing mouth and a pert uptilted nose. The baby was black-haired with her Daddy's almond eyes.

Victor already had a child????

Maybe Victor was the young woman's brother-in-law, I told myself. Or a cousin. Maybe it was just a close family, and that arm around her waist didn't mean they were lovers.

I didn't believe myself for a second. This was a family Victor had never mentioned. Pretty young wife. Beautiful little daughter.

The picture had obviously been done in one of those studios where they dress you up in costume and sepia-tone the prints to make them look old. Victor was in his leather bomber jacket, the same one he had worn when we went flying. His wife was dressed '40s style, her hair tightly curled, a long straight skirt and a white blouse with the sleeves rolled up. The parents looked happy and in love, but the little girl's face was solemn, as if she knew something about the future that her parents couldn't guess.

I turned the picture over. *Giselle et Bianca, Kampong Som.* I decided Giselle was the wife, Bianca the solemn-eyed little girl in the lacy white dress. I turned the picture back, looking at Victor. He looked back at me, smiling. I didn't know anything about him. He had a whole life behind him already, much stranger than I could have imagined. I felt, crushingly, how *young* I was. Compared to a man with a two year old daughter and a wife already in his past, I was really just a kid.

Figure/Ground

I put down the photograph and picked up the day-timer again, skimming through it for references to Giselle and Bianca. Nothing. They seemed to be completely out of his life. Certainly he had never mentioned them to me. I wondered if they had gotten divorced, or if there was an even more tragic story. Car wreck. Plane crash.

Except for the photograph, they might never have existed.

#

I turned back to today's entry and scowled at it.

Jan 31

*5-6 *** New Chair ****

—But I had arrived at a quarter to six, and heard him going out the back door. How could that be if he was at an appointment?

If you're a painter or a psychologist, there's this picture you run across, a simple line drawing of a vase. You stare at it for a few seconds, and suddenly the vase turns into a picture of two faces. It's called a figure/ground reversal, when your basic assumptions flip and you see things totally differently. It happened to me at the exact moment I thought, *What if that wasn't Victor going out the back door?*

Suddenly the elements of the afternoon rearranged themselves like this:

- The door was open for me because somebody else had unlocked it.
- That person wasn't Victor.
- That person hadn't answered me or come to the door because *he wasn't supposed to be in the house.*
- The desk was messy not because Victor had left it that way, but because the intruder had been going through his stuff, searching for something.

I looked again at the desk drawer where the leather wallet had been. The drawer wasn't *broken*; it had a false bottom. The wallet hadn't been sliding *into* it; somebody had been pulling it *out* when I blundered up to the front door and rang the bell.

A burglar had broken into Victor's house, and searched it, and probably stolen things from it. I looked at my watch. 6:32. Any minute now, Victor was going to come home and find he had been robbed. And my fingerprints—the jealous ex-girlfriend's fingerprints—were going to be all over his stuff.

ZING!

My heart kicked like I'd just touched my tongue to a car battery. Oh, boy. Oh, boy.

I ran into the kitchen and grabbed a tea towel and rubbed down the refrigerator handle and the knob on the back door, trying to erase any fingerprints I might have left there. I did the same to the bottle of Chateau Petrus I had pulled out. Then I scampered back to the study, trying to think what all I had touched. Some letters, the day-timer, the picture of Victor with his wife and kid.

Then I heard footsteps starting up the front porch.

Adrenaline took me like a bullet to the heart. I can explain this, I thought. I can tell him exactly how it happened. It was all perfectly natural that I had broken into his house and was standing there with a picture of his ex-wife and daughter in my hand.

Keys jingled and fumbled at the front door.

I grabbed the stuff I knew I had touched, and sprinted wildly for the back door.

Feb 1—Awfully Darn Late
(Hour of the Confused Ex-Girlfriend)

…which is how I come to be sitting here in my bedroom, way past midnight, with a bunch of Victor's stuff.

It was fascinating, looking through all this old stuff, but kind of creepy too. Old photos, old letters, births and deaths…it was like going through the Chan family crypt. Those were real people once, girls anxiously adjusting wedding dresses, little boys digging into birthday cake and looking forward to summer vacation. Couples falling in love or worrying about how to pay the bills. But now there was nothing left of those lives but these scattered scraps of paper, like the bones and hair jumbled in a coffin long after everything else has crumbled away.

*

Who is the woman in the photo?

*

I can't stop looking at this picture, Victor and Giselle and the baby, Bianca. It couldn't have been taken more than a couple of years ago. Victor looks just like he did the day he took me flying.

My family has pictures like this, too. There's one of Mom and Dad and me at the Tall Ships Festival two years ago. I was in my Goth phase at the time, but I'm eating an ice-cream cone with the goofiest smile on my face. Even Mom is relaxed and laughing. Just like Victor and Giselle: we all look happy as clams. None of us knew what was coming, except for little Bianca. Poor kid. I wonder if she ever knew her Dad.

Oh, hell. Now I'm crying.

Feb 1, Next Morning
(Hour of the First Cup of Coffee)

Man. I just read over what I wrote last night. I sure get sentimental after midnight.

Behaved like a complete moron yesterday. No more of that. Today I'm going to go to school like a good girl, make all my classes, try not to fall even further behind. Tonight, after Mom goes to the hospital, I will return Victor's stuff. I looked up the Eight Ancestors; it's a restaurant in Chinatown. It will be a nice, crowded, public place; if I drop by, neither one of us will make a scene. I'll give Victor his things, say I'm sorry, and we'll call it quits for good. Obviously V has a lot of ghosts in his life, and doesn't need things complicated by a 12th Grade sketch artist with delusions of grandeur.

It's morning again, and my head is clear. Mom's right: you can only go so far pretending you live in a soap opera. There's always a reasonable explanation for things. Victor's a busy guy who shouldn't have been hanging out with me anyway, and I shouldn't have let him believe I was in college. The Chagall painting in his study is an imitation, that's all, and I should be flattered to see it there. The mark on my arm was just a spider bite, and V dumped me because he got tired of me. It sucks, but that's the way things happen in real life. The guy had a wife and child. What would there be to

27.

Crowfall at twilight
Black-winged, they settle in trees,
Wires. One is missing.

28

hold him to a girl he never *quite* kissed?

I'll live.

Feb 1, Night
(Chinese New Year—Year of the Ram)
Chinatown

Sometimes, there are worlds hidden behind other worlds. Columbus, Magellan, Cook—they spent years in stinking wooden ships to discover their secret continents. I got to mine in 80 minutes, BART to Richmond station, then the bus to Jackson Street: Chinatown!

I hadn't realized it was Chinese New Year until I heard the grinning chorus of *Gong Hay Fat Choy!* as each new passenger squeezed onto the bus. Middle-aged women chatted back and forth in Cantonese, shaking their heads and emphasizing each point by rattling the handles of their bulging plastic shopping bags. By the time we got to Chinatown proper the bus was packed. Those of us getting out at the Jackson Street stop were shot from the back doors like seeds squeezed out of a lemon. I was running late—it was already close to eight o'clock, and I was worried I might miss Victor.

Chinatown was jammed. Masses of people jostled happily on both sides of the street, spilling over the sidewalk and into the gutters. Light pulsed up through the fat body of the jolly neon Buddha over the Double Fortune Butcher Shop (*Positively No Gambling!*) It was incredibly noisy—people arguing and laughing and shouting across the street, traffic honking to get by, bicycle bells, drums and cymbals and horns from a distant parade, and the constant pop and snap of firecrackers, which people would light in packs and toss into the air, so the whole night smelled like gunpowder.

Normally I don't feel tall, but in Chinatown I was *tall.* You couldn't miss it, either, as people were constantly bumping into me, cutting around me as they hurried down the street, jostling me with shopping bags as they bustled out of apothecary shops or greengrocers, or knocking into me as they jumped out of the street to avoid getting run over. When I got to the Eight Ancestors restaurant I was almost flattened as the big glass doors burst open and spilled out a loud family, laughing and quarreling. The crowd took me backwards until a hard shove and a burst of Cantonese stopped me in my tracks

"Hey!" I shouted, spinning around. "Keep your freaking hands...to..."

I trailed off. The guy who had pushed me looked like a hitman from a John Woo movie. He was wearing a shiny black suit, mirror shades, and a tie with laughing Mickey Mouse heads down the length of it. He had a one-piece cell phone curled around one ear and two friends at his side. They were standing in front of a long black limousine at the curb as if they had orders to execute anyone who scratched the paintwork. The one I had backed into cocked his head, waiting for me to keep talking. Someone let off a Roman candle in the street. Bright chunks of flame moved like slow bullets across his mirrored shades.

I gulped. "Sorry," I muttered, and I hurried through the restaurant door.

Incredibly, it was even louder inside, a roar of conversation and clinking cutlery and waiters wheeling trolleys of food between the tables. The place smelled of steamed crabs and sizzling garlic and black bean sauce, and most of all like cigarettes. It's against the law to smoke inside a restaurant in California, but I wasn't in California anymore—I was in Chinatown on New Year's Eve, and the rules were different. Smoke hung in clouds, drifting up from between the fingers of laughing middle-aged Chinese. The restaurant was basically an enormous open area crowded with tables. There must have been five or six hundred customers, and dozens of red-uniformed waiters. I scanned the room for Victor, eyes watering from cigarette smoke, and I noticed a curious thing.

A man was making his way forward from the very back of the restaurant. Where he passed, silence fell like a shadow. One or two people saw him, and nodded in respect, but these were rare. The other diners didn't even seem to notice him. They would pause, groping for words, but they didn't notice they had been caught in a moving pocket of silence, any more than a blade of grass would notice the shadow of a cloud drifting by. And then the man would be past, and their talk or laughter would burst out again. He was heading for the door, coming directly toward me.

I stepped to one side as he passed the nearest table. Our eyes met, and stillness closed over me as if I were falling down a well. What I could see of the room began to shrink. As it shrank, the noise faded: a dim roar; subsiding; then only the voices of the nearest table were left. Then they died too, and there was only the old man and the sound of my breathing. Then there was just his face, and the sound of my heart. Then I fell into the pupil of his eye. My heartbeat slowed, and stopped.

In that intense stillness, the old man laughed. "You have a good eye," he said. "Someone has taught you to see."

*

—*Cathy, come here. When I squirt your mother's plant mister into a beam of sunshine, look what happens! Rainbows!*

*

—*I spy, with my little eye, something that is…pink!*

*

—*Good! Red plus blue makes purple. And red plus yellow makes…?*

*

—*Touch with your eyes, Cathy. Handle things with them, so you can tell by looking if they are rough, or slick, or damp and soft, like mushrooms.*
You have to cry with your hand, and laugh with it, and let it sing.
You have to see with your heart. You have to see with your heart.

*

The restaurant roared and chattered around me. I turned around, dazed, but the old man had gone. I couldn't say how tall he was, or what he had been wearing. He had a long white beard split into three forks, I remembered that; and his voice wasn't a sound you listened to, but a feeling you woke up from: like a memory, or a dream.

*

Someone grabbed me tightly around the arm and pushed me back toward the restaurant doors. It was Victor.

"What the *hell* are you doing here?" he hissed. "I thought I told you to stay away from me?"

"It's nice to see you, too, Victor." I jerked my arm away from his. "I see your manners haven't changed."

"Get out of here. I'm not joking. I don't want you seen with me."

31.

I tried to slap him but he caught my hand. I glared at him. "That was rude."

He dragged me through the restaurant doors. Outside it was getting colder. Coils of steam rose up into the glow of the streetlights, leaking from the mouths of people laughing and shouting. The crowd split around us as we stood on the sidewalk glaring at one another. "*Rude!*" Victor said. "No, breaking into people's houses is rude."

"I never—"

"Robbed me? Give me a break, Cathy. How did you know I would be here? You found the appointment in the missing pages from my day-timer, that's how. Whoever robbed me yesterday left all my money and took a chocolate bar," he added. "Who does that sound like to you?"

I was furious, but being 100% guilty slowed me down for a sec. "But—"

"I want that day-timer back," he continued relentlessly. "I want my pictures back, I want my jade back."

"I never took your jade—"

"Shut up, Cathy! I want my stuff back, and then I want you out of my life."

Grasping at straws, I drew myself up and yelled the first thing that came into my head. "You jerk, *what did you do to my* **arm**?"

Victor let go of me like he'd been electrocuted. His mouth worked.

"Oh, my God," I whispered. "You really *did* do something to me."

We stared at one another.

"Hey!" Someone yelled at Victor in Cantonese. It was the hard-faced man with the mirror shades and the Mickey Mouse tie. The limousine had left and one of his friends was gone. The other was standing next to him with a lighter and a couple of packs of firecrackers, each about the size of an 8-pack of crayons.

"What's he saying?" I asked.

Victor shrugged. "I don't speak Chinese."

"Hey, Banana-Man," Mickey Mouse said, in English this time. "Your girlfriend's cute." He smiled. It wasn't a nice smile. "Want to share?"

Something in Victor went still, as if all his anger at me had suddenly condensed into something cool, hard, and smooth as a bullet. "You want to eat your own teeth?"

32.

Mickey Mouse waggled a finger at him reprovingly. "Hey—you better mind your manners, Banana-Man." I thought, *You aren't paying attention, dude.* Couldn't he feel how dangerous Victor had become? Apparently not. He glanced at his buddy.

The friend flicked his lighter and touched it to the fuse on his pack of firecrackers. "*Gong Hay Fat Choy!*" he yelled, and he threw them at me.

Time slowed down.

I don't mean that like a figure of speech. I mean that next to Victor, time slowed down. Seconds stretched out like molasses creeping down the side of a jar. Further away, on the other side of the street, people were hurrying along at their usual rate: but here, close to Victor, I could see the individual firecrackers kindling one by one. Sparks spilled out, dancing slowly from fuse to fuse as the whole pack tumbled lazily through the air. I had time to look over and see reflected fire spit and flicker in Mickey Mouse's mirrored eyes. A smile started to inch up his face. Around us, the shoes of passing pedestrians drifted gently up and down, as if lifted by slow ocean currents.

In all this dream-slow world, only Victor was moving normally. He caught the two packs of firecrackers out of the air, one in each hand, and jumped toward Mickey Mouse. Mickey's eyes began to widen. In absurd slow motion, he tried to raise one arm to shield himself, but he had barely started to flinch when Victor drove an elbow into his nose. It broke with a wet crack, like a green branch snapping. Mickey started to topple ponderously back into the street. The further he got from Victor, the quicker he fell; when Victor jumped over to his buddy, Mickey collapsed at nearly normal speed.

Victor grabbed the second thug's hands, wrapped them around the firecrackers, and pressed them into his stomach. His eyes went round and his mouth widened into an O as he looked down. Sparks gleamed and spat from between his fingers. Each individual firecracker went off like a bullet, with its own clear bang. Jerks and shudders spread under the guy's hands, rippling his torso, making his head wobble and his arms flop in slow underwater jerks. His knees buckled, his legs gave way, and he drifted to the sidewalk.

Victor spun and looked at me, wild and grinning and smelling like gunpowder. At that instant I felt certain he had killed men before. You could read it in the way he stood over the two fallen bodies, easy in his victory. He laughed, and I wondered how many men he had killed, and I thought it was probably a lot.

Do you remember the first time you knew you were going to die? I was five...

*

Time sped up.

*

(continued over)

Victor was standing beside me, no longer smiling. He had folded up that hunter's grin like a knife and tucked it away. Blood was welling between his blackened fingers. He glanced down at the guy twitching on the sidewalk at his feet. "Happy New Year." He took my hand. "Come on. Let's get out of here."

"What about him? I think he's hurt bad."

Victor shrugged. "People die. I just don't want you to be one of them."

I let Victor pull me along the sidewalk. Already I was less sure of what I had seen. I was beginning to wonder if I were sick, or drugged. The crowds closed behind us, hiding the flattened thugs. Quickly Victor turned one corner, went half a block, turned down another alley, and hustled us along until we came out into a crowded plaza. The crowd noise was very loud—we had found the parade I'd heard earlier, and the air was split with crashing cymbals. "Where are we?" I yelled.

"Portsmouth Square."

"I need to sit down," I shouted, putting my back against a building. He nodded and I let myself slip down. I just wanted a second to catch my breath and clear my head.

Victor squatted beside me. "Sorry about that," he said. "I lost my temper."

"Sorry for shouting at me, or for half-killing those guys?"

"I'm not really a great date sometimes, am I?" Victor reached out, ever so hesitantly, and cupped my cheek in his hand. "I wish you could have met my sister. She would have liked you."

"So introduce me."

"She died," he said. "She… Never mind. Look, Cathy, I'm sorry about everything. I like you a lot. More than you could guess. But it just won't … It's bad luck to get mixed up with the men in my family. We have a bad habit

34.

✱ I was watching a Star Trek rerun and one of the characters got zapped with a Death Ray and somehow I just got it! He was never coming back, and that would happen to me someday, I started crying and I couldn't stop. Finally Mom asked what was the matter but I couldn't tell her. It was too big, this huge dark thing in my chest. I kept crying and crying until Mom started getting mad so I said my head hurt and she gave me some medicine and put me to bed. I held it in all the way through story, but when they were gone I lay there in my bed holding my hand over my mouth & my whole body shaking with these huge terrible sobs. Then the TV downstairs went off, and my parents went to bed, and my Dad turned off the light in the hallway so the little bar of light under my door went dark. I had a hamster back then called Georgette, I could hear her rustling in ~~because~~ the darkness, and I thought about how that would sound in an empty room, if I was dead, and how nobody would feed Georgette or play with her, or if they did it wouldn't be me, it would be a stranger, because the world would go on but there would be no me in it, I would be like a poster you take off the wall & throw away: or the empty space on the wall where the poster used to hang. These little rustles from the hamster cage, going on as if I wasn't there, as if I was dead already, and the night went on forever.

35.

of disappearing."

"I noticed," I said dryly.

"Cathy, you're just a kid, and I'm not a good guy to get involved with. There's a lot of stuff you don't know."

His hand was warm against my cheek. I said, "You could tell it to me."

Gently he pushed one strand of hair back from my eyes. "I almost think I could." Time slowed. He looked at me then, and I thought maybe he was going to kiss me, and I thought maybe I would let him.

*

My cell phone rang.

Damn!

Victor stood up. I flipped open the phone. "Hullo?"

"It's Carla Beckman, right?"

"Is that Emma?"

"Carla Beckman, Intrepid Biotech Associate Scientist."

"I don't really care about her right now," I said. "Listen, I've got to go—"

"She's dead," Emma said.

"Carla's dead?"

"What was that?" Victor said sharply. I waved him off, trying to hear Emma over the roar and chatter of the crowd.

"Some campers found her body this morning washed up on a beach," Emma said.

"Drowned?"

"Possibly. The two bullets to the stomach probably didn't help either."

"Oh, my God! How did you find this out?"

"Insider sources from the police department. I read it in the paper, dummy. Ready for the kicker?"

I hunkered down with my phone, trying to hear her through the chaos of Chinese New Year crashing around me. "Hit me."

"Body was found just south of Monterey—about ten minutes from that place your boyfriend took us for lunch on our memorable plane trip."

"Oh, my God." I thought back to what I'd seen in Victor's day-timer, a rash of appointments with Carla last week, and nothing since.

"If I saw your friend Victor, I would run," Emma said.

I gulped and looked up. I couldn't see Victor. I jumped to my feet. He had melted into the crowds cheering and clapping in Portsmouth Square, and he was gone.

Part II
Feb 2, Sunday Morning
(Hour of the Really Creepy Thought)

Woke to the smell of gunpowder still faint on my pillow, and the memory of firecrackers sparking in slow motion. Mom had to try three times before she could get me out of bed. "If you're trying to convince me you're not doing drugs, it isn't working."

Q: So, *what if I* am *on drugs?*

Feb 2, Afternoon
(Hour of the Mall Food Court)

"The needle mark," Emma said, eyes widening. "You think Victor shot you up?"

It was Sunday and we were at the mall. "I know he did something to my arm, and time keeps going slow on me."

"Probably just adrenaline. Like when a character in a book is in danger and his Life Flashes Before His Eyes."

"Maybe," I said, not believing it.

We ambled over to Radio Shack. "Thirty-thirty still intact," Emma reported cheerfully. Emma's goal was to make $30 million by age 30, which she planned to get by selling voice-recognizing cell phones to the untapped Chinese market. Every couple of weeks she stopped by a Radio Shack or Fry's Electronics to convince herself that voice rec. software was still lame enough that she wouldn't get scooped during the three and a half years she planned to be at M.I.T.

"What are you going to do after 30/30?" I said, angling toward the food court. "Rule the world, I suppose?"

"A girl needs a dream."

We found a table at the food court and sat down. Emma dug a sheaf of papers out of her backpack. "Did you know Victor's company got bought out a few weeks ago?" She passed me a couple of press releases she'd printed off the internet. "Taken over by P'eng-Lai Pharmaceuticals. Lay-offs expected."

"Do you think Victor got fired?"

"Why would he care if he's stinking rich?"

"Hm… I guess the money wouldn't matter. But this happened right around the time he started getting weird and not wanting to see me."

"He was up to something in the lab," Emma said. "I can just feel it."

"What do they make at Intrepid Biotech, anyway?"

"Nothing."

"What?"

Emma shrugged. "They've been doing R&D—they really are working on an anti-cancer vaccine, actually, but they've only been at it nine years. Naturally they don't have a *product* yet."

"*Nine years?*"

Emma rolled her eyes. "Honestly, biotech is a business nightmare. There's plenty of companies that burn money for fifteen years and *never* get a product."

"Why would anyone start a company that—"

"Potential payout. Think of your average product. Snow-blowers, say. You can sell them in Alaska but not in Florida, to home-owners but not people who live in apartments. With me so far?"

"Yeah."

Emma looked up from the sheaf of Intrepid press releases. "So the market for bio-tech is, People Who Don't Want To Get Sick and Die."

Ah. "Big market."

"What do you think we would pay for a vaccine against lung cancer, or Alzheimers, or a pill that would stop heart disea—?" Her hands flew up to cover her mouth, the one Chinese mannerism she had never broken. "Oh, my God, Cathy. I just wasn't thinking."

"It's okay," I said.

*

My dad painted birds.

"*That's it, Cathy—fat over lean, just like that. You know, in my youth, back before they invented the printing press and dirt was young, I used to do these awful things, nightmarish paintings full of what I thought was this very profound anger, this great disillusionment. Boy, nobody's disillusioned like a twenty-one year old who doesn't know a damn thing yet. So I did these paintings and everyone was real respectful*"— "*Even Mom?*"—"*Almost everyone, I should say. So I got paid good money, even won some prizes…But then I had a kiddo, and all that anger just seemed stupid.*"

*

"I'm *so* sorry!" Emma fumbled with her papers. "Um—I'm just going to get a bite to eat. Want anything?"

My eyes were stinging. I wiped them roughly and pulled a peanut-butter sandwich out of my purse. "My body is a temple." The truth is, we're too broke for me to buy food at the mall. Mom's got more important things to spend her money on. Like gin.

Emma got a Taco Combo and bought me a Coke anyway. "Thanks," I said.

I pulled up my sleeve. The needle mark had faded to where I couldn't see it anymore. "Could Victor have been trying out some new miracle cure on me? Maybe he was giving me an experimental cancer vaccine."

"I'm pretty sure your average FDA-approved human drug trial doesn't involve knocking out the lab-tech's girlfriend and shooting her up without her consent. More likely he was cooking up some killer street drug—testing it for side effects, maybe, or addictiveness."

Ugh. "I liked 'cancer vaccine' better. Besides, your idea is way too risky— knock me out and shoot me up? If he can afford a Chagall, he could just hire some wino to get needled up like a pin-cushion, and monitor him in a Scary Drug Dungeon somewhere."

"I wonder what it costs to build one of those?" Emma mused. "I suppose the modern crime lord rents, for superior flexibility."

The food court was starting to fill up. A tired young woman dragged a snivelling little girl to the table next to us and started grimly feeding her French fries. The toddler ate messily, between snuffles, stuffing each fry into her mouth with her whole grubby fist. "I wonder if Victor's wife and kid are in a food court right now," I said. "Giselle and Bianca."

"Only if they have malls in Cambodia."

"What?"

Emma licked taco juice from her fingers. "After you called me, I googled some of the stuff, including the name on the back of the photograph. Kampong Som is a beach town in Cambodia. More often called Sihanoukville, after the king or general or whatever who led Cambodia to independence from French Indochina right before the Viet Nam war."

So Giselle would have been the daughter of a French businessman, or

40.

diplomat maybe? Check that grand-daughter. Or maybe she met Victor there
when he was backpacking…some time between learning to fly airplanes in Junior
High, and opening up a secret molecular biology lab.

Sheesh.

I thought about Victor's jade charm, the one he accused me of having stolen,
and wondered if it was a souvenir from their trip to Cambodia. Something Giselle
had given him. "I was looking at the wedding invitation later. Very fancy. I
wonder if her family came over from France."

Emma frowned. "What do you mean, you were looking at it *later?*

"Oh, you know," I said vaguely. "Hey—how was your taco?"

Her eyes narrowed. "Cathy, you didn't *take something from his house,* did you?"

"Sometimes they make them kinda greasy," I mumbled.

"Cathy!"

"Someone was coming. I panicked."

"Great." Emma rolled her eyes. "Well, obviously that was Very Wrong," she
said sternly, "—but since it happened, show me what you got."

"Oh, Emma—I'd never *dream* of making you an *accessory.*"

"Very funny. Show me what you got, or I'll call the cops and turn you in."

"What makes you think I brought any of this stuff with me?"

"You don't like figuring things out if you think I can save you the effort."

"I hate you," I said. I mean that, I mean seriously... heeheehee

"Plus you brought your school backpack to the mall on a Sunday, dummy."

Busted.

Emma laughed at me as I wiped off the table with my sleeve and spread out
the loot I'd pilfered from Victor's study. She picked through the stuff greedily,
lingering over the old newspaper clipping and the picture of Victor and Giselle.
She didn't miss Victor, god knows, and she thought I was an idiot for ever going
to his house, but that girl does love a puzzle. She turned her attention to a little
envelope with a scrap of paper inside with a red lipstick kiss on it. She held the
paper distastefully between the tips of her fingers, like something that needed to
be wiped down with disinfectant. "Eww."

"I know."

"This wasn't from you?"

41.

PhoneGirrrrl

42.

"Emma! You think I'd send him a little kissy face?"

She looked at me over the tops of her glasses.

"I don't wear Pop-Tart red! I wouldn't be caught dead wearing this."

"Carla was," Emma said. Which kind of took the fun out of the conversation.

Emma dropped the paper and picked up the pages from Victor's day-timer. "Carla's phone number!"

"Yeah. I'm not sure what the other numbers here are about," I said, pointing to where he had written 1 4?5? 9 2?3?

Emma's eyes narrowed. "Do you have a cell phone with you?" I nodded. "Pass it over."

"Where's yours?" I said, digging mine out of my purse.

"Hang on." Emma took my phone, consulted the day-timer and punched in Carla's number, 408 236-2161.

"Emma!"

(A) — Shows Good Initiative in problem solving.

"What, like she's going to answer?" Emma turned the phone so I could just hear Carla's answering service message.

A recorded voice said, "If you wish to retrieve your messages, please enter your four-digit access code now."

Emma tapped the piece of paper from the day-timer. "He was trying to hack her access code so he could listen to her phone messages."

A+ "Omigod! Emma, that's brilliant!"

She grinned. "I am PhoneGrrl, remember? Victor must have spied on her sometime when she was picking up her messages. He's got her access code narrowed down to four possibilities for you." She looked up expectantly.

"You expect me to break into her message system?"

"Duh!"

The light dawned. "That's why you borrowed my phone," I said. "You didn't want the phone company logs showing you making calls into Carla's mailbox, you cow."

"You know me too well." Zero signs of shame and remorse. "I think we should probably let you do all the illegal stuff, really. You are the crazy obsessed ex-girlfriend, after all. Juries love that. Cute young suburban girl is drawn into a Web of Intrigue—"

"Oh, shut up."

I got the right access code on the second try.

We listened to the messages twice: a reminder that Carla was scheduled for a meeting with her bosses (from which she would never return alive!), and the sound of Victor's desperate voice, begging her not to tell anyone about a secret project he was working on.

"Good lord," Emma breathed.

"Okay. Let's think this through," I said. "Point One: Intrepid Biotech gets bought out. There's new management coming in."

"Victor's worried," Emma said. "He's got something going in the lab."

"That's pretty clear in the phone message. *If you go to Intrepid now, they'll just laugh at you. As for your "auction it to Genentech and let them bid" idea, that's just going to get us both fired.*"

"She decides to do it anyway," Emma said. "She confronts Victor, like you did last night. And then she disappears," Emma said, slowing down. "And drowns. And gets shot."

We looked at one another.

"I don't like that story," I said. "That's a scary story."

I dialed Carla's number and put in the access code and listened to her messages again. Somehow hearing Victor's desperate voice on her answering service made the whole thing seem far more real.

Emma looked at me over the tops of her little round glasses. "Cathy, promise me you are going to stay completely out of this."

"Are you kidding?" I said. "You think I'm crazy? You think I want to get shot and drowned and stuff?"

"So you're not going to go poking around Victor's house—"

"No!"

"—or checking his airplane to see if it's still in the hangar—"

"God, you're right! I bet he took the plane! Even if the cops had his driver's license, it might be a while before they thought to check for the pl—"

"CATHY!"

"Oops. Sorry." I wrapped my lips around my Coke straw and blew meek little bubbles into it. "It's not like I was going to—"

"Promise!"

"I promise," I said. *I had my toes crossed!*

44

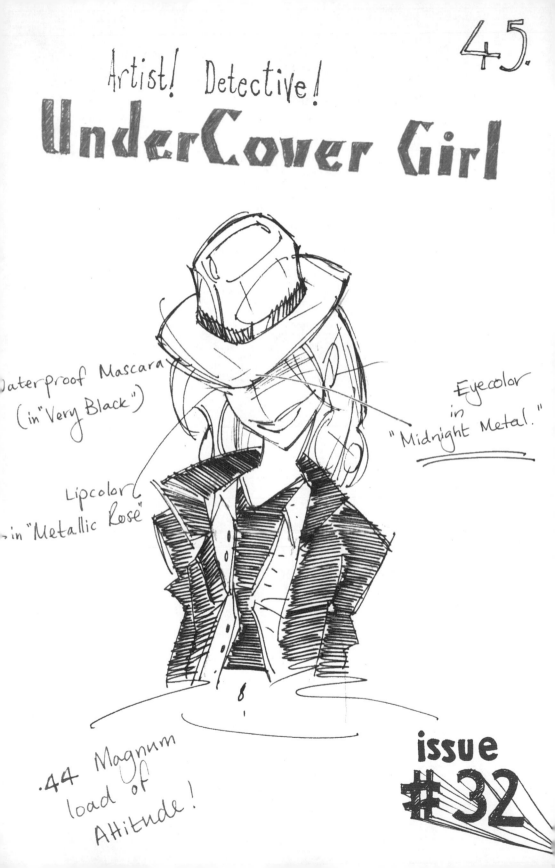

Feb 3, Morning
(Hour of the Famous Last Words)

Obviously, though, there wouldn't be any harm in going to Chinatown to do a little research on that stolen jade pendant.

Feb 3, Evening
(Hour of the Paper Bird)

Back from Chinatown. Still alive. Deeply freaked.

The further in I go, the weirder it gets.

*

Got home from school, ignored Mom's questions about homework, and found an old sketch of Victor wearing his pendant. I painted a big version in my sketch pad to show while I was asking questions.

Detective ArtGrrl makes the rounds of her informants, carrying her bullet-proof sketch pad and a .44 Magnum load of Attitude. She's tricked out in gun-metal grey eyeliner and sweat-proof mascara black as powder burns.

ArtG: Here's the 411, see? Finger the perp who snagged the loot, & I'll make the collar, see.

Witness: What?

ArtG: <sigh…>

*

Mom took the car to work, so I was stuck doing BART again. Cold and gray outside: winter sun a pale smudge, sinking fast in a tired sky. When we pulled into Richmond station, BART cops were clearing out a smattering of panhandlers, sweeping them into the chilly blue evening. They drifted over to the bus shelters, all the Usual Suspects:

- Veteran Who Will Work For Food.
- Fat old Chinese man folding paper flowers, selling them for change.
- Goth chick in a dirty down-filled ski-vest three sizes too small. Narrow face, dark rings around the eyes. I wondered which drugs she was doing with her panhandling money, and whether Victor made them.

*

46.

6:03 when I got off the bus on Jackson Street. It was already dark. Winos stretched across the busy sidewalk. Bustling crowds stepped over them and didn't look down. Girls were getting off retail shifts—young dudes in flash suits were talking on cell phones. Short old ladies labored under plastic shopping bags that bulged w/produce. Everyone Chinese except me & the winos.

On Grant Street, I found a promising jewelry store called Jade Empire.

ArtG: <holds up painting of pendant> "Excuse me, do you know—"

Clerk: <frowning> "You here buy?"

ArtG: "Not today, I don't think."

Clerk: ☹

ArtG: "I was just wondering—"

Clerk: "No. Try Treasure Palace."

ArtG: ☹

Nobody at Treasure Palace spoke any English at all.

THIRTY MINUTES LATER I was really feeling like a stupid kid from the 'burbs. Didn't these people understand that real Americans should speak a real American language from a real down-home part of America, like England? But somehow it turned out that the real America was even bigger and stranger than the one you see on MTV.

I drifted down the street (discouraged + hungry), but I only had a $5, and I needed half that for bus & BART fare home. I ducked into the Sun Lok Bakery. Nobody admitted knowing English. I pointed at what I hoped would be a barbecue pork bun. It wasn't.

I headed back into the chilly night, chewing grimly. Every shop door was open, letting a different smell into the street: hot dough and barbecue sauce from the Sun Lok; dust & cheap paper at the Hundred Dragon used book store next door; cod and trout and squid, damp gleaming slabs of them, laid out on ice at Wu's fish market. Used clothes one door after that, cheap sundresses and polyester pants from Hong Kong, stinking of mothballs and cedar.

I turned down Ross Alley and walked the length of the Golden Gate Fortune Cookie Factory. The alley door was open. Steam billowed out of it into the night air. On the ground, white flour footprints walked into the alley, ghost steps that

◆ JADE EMPIRE ◆

faded into the night.

The smell of steam and cookie dough gave way to incense at the end of the block, seeping around the doorway of the

My Jong Trading Co.

MY JONG TRADING CO

Through the window, strange treasures: incense sticks & chess pieces & trays of jewelry, Buddhas in jade and brass and ivory, with big bellies and long, droopy ears. Old leather-covered books, dull under a layer of dust. Jars of dice and dominoes and mah-jong tiles, and in front of them all, my own pale reflection, drifting like a ghost in the glass.

A brass bell chimed as I walked through the door. Inside, the air was warm and thick and smelled of incense and pipe tobacco. I wound my way between stacks of books and serpent statues and shiny black lacquered furniture with dragon-clawed feet. I headed for a coil of smoke drifting up from the back of the store. Squeezing behind a set of bamboo screens, I found myself in front of a glass display tray crammed with rings, lockets, pocket watches, pins, stamps, seals, and other shiny things. A fat marmalade cat lay draped across the glass counter; behind it, a grey-haired Chinese woman perched on a lacquered stool, smoking a long-stemmed clay pipe.

I flipped open my sketchbook and held up my painting of Victor's pendant. "My boyfriend had this charm," I said, speaking slowly and distinctly. "Can you tell me about it?"

The shopkeeper lifted the cat's tail and tapped on the glass counter with the stem of her pipe, indicating a box of jade charms, none of which looked anything like Victor's. "Maybe you like?"

"No, thanks."

She shrugged and jammed the pipe back in her mouth.

"Kuei tablet," a new voice said. I jumped and spun around. There, tucked in the corner, was an old, old Chinese man. He had a round, wrinkled face mostly hidden in white hair, with white side whiskers and a white mustache and a long, trailing white beard. He was dressed in a baggy, patched robe with a pattern of bamboo leaves on it. The table in front of him held stacks and stacks of what looked like paper money, but the money was blue and red, and instead of a dead

48.

President, it showed a chubby wise-eyed toddler with a giant fish in his lap. The white-haired old man was folding two of these bills together, tucking and pinching them into a curious shape.

"Wah!" said the shopkeeper. She bowed so deeply to the old man, you would have thought he was an emperor, or a saint. He smiled and said something in Chinese; she bowed again and hurried into the back of the store. They must have had a kitchen there, because I could hear tea-making sounds: tap-water filling a kettle, and the *whump* of a gas stove coming on.

I stared more closely at the old man. "I know you! I saw you at the Richmond BART station, making paper flowers!"

"Must have kuei tablet, to see Emperor," the old man wheezed. "Or—for Emperor see *you*." He smiled, making his face crinkle up into a mass of worn creases, like a map that had been mis-folded ten-thousand times. "We same, you and me. We *meddle*." All the time he spoke, he kept folding the colorful money, making the bills squeak and rustle. The big marmalade cat pricked up its ears, watching the old man work. "We *meddlers*."

He held up a paper bird, sparrow-sized, but lurid with the colors of the strange money. The ginger cat rolled to its feet, ears pricked and quivering. The old man flicked his fingers and the paper bird hopped into the air.

Time faltered.

I heard the hiss of a kettle in the back room. Hairs rose on the cat's neck. I felt my heartbeat, slow as a long wave breaking in my chest. Loops and strings of gray smoke hung coiling in the air. I watched them pull around the bird's shiny wings: and snap: and spin slowly in its wake.

*

The cat sprang off the counter with a yowl. The paper bird dipped for all the world as if it were flicking its wings, and darted off behind the bamboo screens. Behind it, the frustrated cat landed belly down on the bald head of a bronze Buddha and hung there, scrabbling in a most undignified fashion, until it slid slowly backwards over the Enlightened One's tummy, and landed with a thump on the oriental rug. The cat immediately strolled away, denying he had ever looked ridiculous.

A bead curtain at the back of the room rustled as the shopkeeper returned

49.

carrying a black-lacquered tray with an iron teapot and two small cups. She offered tea to the old man. He took it gratefully and sipped. "You want audience with Emperor?" he said, nodding at my painting of Victor's pendant.

"With the Emperor?" I felt like the cat—in way, way over my head, and making more of a fool of myself with every passing minute.

The old man grinned. "Say, with one who give tablet."

Who the heck would that be? Victor, or someone else? What if it was some kind of Fu Manchu…? Maybe the "Emperor" was like a Chinese Godfather, running opium into America. I imagined myself dragged into some dockside dungeon and thrown at the feet of an Evil Kingpin in silk robes who would subject me to exotic tortures for having stolen Victor's stuff.

This is what Mom means when she says I have an Artistic Temperament.

The shopkeeper gave me a cup of tea. It was cloudy green, fragrant and a little sad: the smell of damp autumn leaves burning in the distance. Obviously, there was no *way* was I going to drink it. It could be drugged, or poisoned, or, or …well, I wasn't going to drink it.

The old man smiled. "Old friend of mine, once offered very great post. Great honor. He say no. 'I would rather be a turtle, wagging my tail in the mud!'" The old man chuckled. "Dangerous, for small person to meddle with great. Wiser stay home, and wag your tail in the mud!" He tilted his head, studying me. "But… maybe you too young to be wise?"

"Sounds like me."

The old man nodded. "Wait little bit. I go find man with kuei tablet." He huffed and wheezed to his feet, then paused. "When he comes, I think better not say how old, Painting Girl."

"I shouldn't say how old I am?" I said, mystified.

"And not birth moon!"

"Moon? What? You mean my birthday?"

He clucked and held one finger across his bearded lips—*shhhh!*—then shuffled through the curtain into the back of the store.

The Man Who Gives Tablets was coming, but I wasn't to tell him how old I was, or what my birthday was? *What?*

A loud, paper-rattling sound came from the back room, as if someone were

50.

trying to read a Sunday newspaper in a high wind.

The shopkeeper steadily refused to turn around and investigate. "Tea good, okay?" she said, raising her voice over the sound of crackling paper.

"Peachy." I lifted my cup to my lips and pretended to sip, wishing she would leave the room so I could pour the stuff into a dragon-wreathed porcelain vase I had spotted in the corner.

The paper-folding sounds faded to a series of flaps and rustles. There was a moment of silence, followed by a loud braying noise.

"What the heck was *that*?"

The shopkeeper looked at me, politely puzzled.

There was another short bray, followed by a sort of whinny. "Do you have a pony in your kitchen?" I said loudly.

"Ah, yes!" the shopkeeper said. She nodded vigorously, tamping down the tobacco in the bowl of her pipe and reaching into the pockets of her polyester slacks. "Is wind," she added.

"The wind?" I repeated incredulously.

She dug a silver cigarette lighter out of her pocket. "Wind. Yes."

There was another whinny from the back room, after which I distinctly heard the clip-clop of hooves walking across a linoleum floor.

The shopkeeper flicked her lighter and sucked a leaf of yellow flame down into the bowl of her pipe. Flakes of tobacco shone like hot wires. I heard the back door open. Slow hoofbeats clattered outside and dwindled into the dim night.

"Now what?" I said.

Strings of smoke trickled out between the shopkeeper's grinning teeth. "Now wait."

We waited.

This is crazy, I thought. I should go. I promised Emma I wasn't going to get any more involved in Victor's mysterious life. For all I knew, that old man was off to fetch a gang of white slavers, who would pop a bag over my head and ship me to some drug dealer's harem in Singapore. Or, more likely, he was on his way to a soup kitchen, where some long-suffering social worker would pick him up and detain him for mandatory psychiatric evaluation.

"You got dead," the shopkeeper said.

"What?"

"See in eye." She held her pipe by the bowl and tapped her chest with the stem. "Empty heart makes empty eye. You got dead, yes?"

"Yeah." I looked away and sipped my tea before I remembered that I wasn't supposed to do that. The sad taste of burning leaves whispered inside me. Of autumn rain.

"Okey-dokey." The woman bustled over to the table where the old man had been sitting. "You need hell money!" She held up a $100 note. It looked exactly like money from Singapore or Malaysia or Burma, except instead of a President or King, it showed a bald toddler riding a burning half-tiger/half-horse, and the words **Hell Bank Note** were written in English at the top.

"I need Hell money?" I said. "Of course I do. Naturally. Why?"

"You need money. I need money. *Gwai*—dead people—gwai need money also."

"Why?"

She shrugged. "Buy gwai t'ing: gwai food, gwai clothes. Also: go in Heaven." The shopkeeper looked at me as if I wasn't the pointiest pin in the cushion. "You t'ink *gwai* go Heaven free?" She rubbed her fingers together in the Universal Money Gesture. "Heaven guard want pay also. You *gwai*, he need Hell money. You take." When I didn't move, she impatiently peeled off a few hundreds and thrust them at me. "Take!"

"What am I supposed to do with this?"

She bustled into the recesses of her shop and returned a moment later with a small iron brazier with a tiny shrine welded to its back: a toy pagoda no bigger than a hibachi. The shopkeeper set it on her back counter. "Okey-dokey! Now fire!"

"You want me to burn the money?"

She rolled her eyes. "How you t'ink you give to *gwai*? Lette'?" she said sarcastically. "Big stamp, get Heaven, I t'ink!"

She was suggesting I burn play money for my dead father, but apparently *I* was the one looking stupid.

Go figure.

I put the stack of Hell money on the brazier grate.

"You t'ink dead now one minute."

"Okay."

"Close eye help sometime."

52.

"Okay, already!"

I closed my eyes and tried to think about my dad. At first I couldn't do it; my head was too busy wondering where Paper-Folding Man had gone, and if he had really been riding a pony, and who he was going to bring back. I wondered why time had been slowing down on me since the day I discovered the needle mark on my arm. This was twice in a couple of days. No: three times. It had happened in the restaurant too—the old Chinese man with the beard combed into three points had passed me, sounds had faded, and everything had gone still, time and the world stopping: empty as the still center of a spinning wheel....

*

...and out of nowhere I remembered coming home from school, grabbing a glass of milk and sticking my head into my father's studio to say *Hi*, like I did every afternoon.

No answer back. Mom out of town that weekend; the house silent with that empty house feeling.

One wall of the studio was windows. Dad needed lots of natural light to paint. I remember the day was bright. Everything was clear. My father was lying on his back on the studio floor. Across his chest was a broad stripe of light, a sunbeam. Motes of dust, floating in the bar of light.

Time broke.

It was like a bridge with a span dropped out. I was stuck on this side: here. Now. On the other side of the break was the moment when I would scream, when my glass of milk would drop from my hand and I would know my father was dead.

Between those two moments: nothing. A gap.

Dust motes hanging in empty light.

*

"Okay. You do good." The shopkeeper handed me her silver lighter. "Now, make offering."

I flicked the lighter and held the flame under the edge of a 100 Yuan note. I could see the flame gulping through the thin paper. A brown stain flowered on its surface. The paper buckled, shrank, and split, letting a tongue of fire through. In another moment the whole stack of notes had caught. Grey wisps of smoke streamed up. There were tears on my cheeks. I handed the shopkeeper her

53.

lighter back. "Thanks," I said.

She gave my hand a brisk squeeze. Together we watched the little stack of hell money burn down. I wiped the tears off my face with the back of my hand and tried to get my composure back. "Okay. Now what?"

The shopkeeper took another drag on her pipe. "You owe me five dollar."

"Oh. I thought—I mean, I just assumed you were giving me…."

She smiled and shook her head.

Of *course* she hadn't been giving me free merchandise.

I had to pay with a check.

*

Clip-clop, clip-clop. Hoofbeats returning. A door banged open at the back of the shop. More miscellaneous braying was slowly drowned out by loud paper-folding noises, as if someone was trying to wrap a donkey in layers of Christmas paper. Or as if—a tingling prickle ran down my spine, remembering the paper bird that had seemed to flick its wings and fly—as if the old man were *folding the donkey up like a map, and sticking it in his pocket.*

The curtain at the back of the room swung aside and a newcomer stepped into the room. His clothes were immaculate but old-fashioned: a long black military jacket, tightly buttoned at the collar, and a black cap on top of his head. The jacket was cinched around his waist with a wide black sash, and stuck into the sash above his left hip was, unmistakably, a long jade tablet shaped exactly like the one Victor used to wear. This one was much larger, about the size of my hand. There was a diamond motif to his accessories—diamond-shaped buttons on his jacket, diamond-shaped diamond cufflinks, and a diamond-shaped medal on his chest, like a badge of honor from some army that no longer existed. The face above the tight collar was proud, disciplined, and unmistakably related to Victor. Physically, he might have been only a few years older than Victor, but he had an air of much greater authority, like that of a four star general, or the Prime Minister of a country at war.

Paper-Folding Man shuffled in behind him.

The Minister looked me over as if I were some faintly unappetizing vegetable that had been left out on a produce stand a couple of days too long. "You must be the girl." His manner was arrogant, but his English was much better than Paper-

A doctor friend of Dad's had just dropped by when I started screaming. He tried to restart Dad's heart, but he couldn't. The ambulance took him away. Dad had written down the wrong number for Mom's hotel, which didn't matter much because he had told me she was in Cancun when she was really in Mazatlan. I never got a chance to talk to her before they cremated him. When we were sprinkling the ashes together she was still so angry at me for not calling her somehow. Angry at him for dying.

Folding Man's. His accent was like Emma's, that Hong Kong/Oxford mix. "What was he like—the one who wore the jade?"

"More polite," I said.

The Minister frowned. Behind his back, Paper-Folding Man smiled in his white beard.

The Minister barked out something in Chinese. Paper-folding Man shrugged and pointed at my sketchbook, which I had left on the counter, still open to the page with the painting of Victor's pendant. The Minister picked up my book and studied the painting. "Ha! Where did you see this?"

"Give that back."

Ignoring me, he flipped through the book until he found one of my sketches of Victor wearing the pendant. In this one I had aged him to about 55 or 60. The Minister stared at it, transfixed, and slowly let out his breath. "So. Of course. Only to be expected," he said. He glanced over at me. "This is the man you saw wearing the jade?"

"Give me my sketchbook back."

"Is this him?"

"Yeah, that's him," I said. I could have explained about how I had aged Victor, but A) I didn't know who the Minister was, or why he was interested in Victor; and B) he was a jerk. "My Dad bought that sketchbook for me. Give it back."

"In a moment." He flipped back a few pages and found a different picture of Victor, this time in his mid-thirties. The Minister frowned and searched more slowly. He found a sketch of Victor just as he appeared today. Turning back a page, he saw a nude self-portrait of me from the waist up, 45 years old, with bags under my eyes and my body widened out with middle-aged spread. "This is you?"

I slapped him in the face and grabbed my book.

The shopkeeper's pipe fell from her astonished mouth. "Wah!"

Paper-Folding Man smirked in his beard.

"You have a good eye," the Minister said, thoughtfully rubbing his cheek. "Good right hand, too."

"Screw you." I shoved the sketchbook into my bag and backed away from the counter.

"Don't go," the Minister said. "I was rude. Forgive me. I am very anxious to find the man who wears the jade." He hesitated. "You may call me Tsao."

"You can call me long distance," I said. "But I'd work on your people skills first."

He started after me. "You don't understand. I gave this man that jade. I have been looking for him a very long time. I have to find him."

"Yeah, well, life's a bitch and then you die."

Turning on my heel, I scampered back through the clutter of the My Jong Trading Co. as fast as I could. As soon as I was outside, I started running. I didn't stop until I was at the bus stop on Grant Street. A #7 had just rolled up and I jumped on, fumbling for my bus fare while looking back over my shoulder. The Minister was striding purposefully up the sidewalk after me. The crowd around him seemed to freeze as he passed. He was only twenty or thirty paces back when, to my intense relief, the bus rumbled forward, leaving him behind. Surrounded by that frozen crowd, he seemed profoundly solitary, like a man standing in a cemetery, alone but for the headstones of the dead.

Feb 3, Way Too Late
(Hour of the Aching Typing Fingers)

Em--

Ongoing adventures of Crazy Cathy's Soap Opera 4 the Terminally Insane: tonight was Big Weird in Little China. See attachment w/ full story.

ALSO--had a thought about the New Chair entry in V's day-timer. New Chair NOT = furniture <duh>. I bet that's an appointment w/ the New Chairman— i.e. new Chairman of Intrepid Biotech, post-takeover.

So: Timeline

Jan 2 Merger announced.

Jan 24-27 3 meetings w/ Carla. "What's gonna happen w/ new guys?!?!"
Either:

- Carla = Victor's accomplice? Or
- Carla discovered V was up to No Good, Or
- Carla was blackmailing V? Maybe she knew Victor was rich? -->

"Give me a cut, or I blow the whistle to the new boss!"

Jan 28 Carla disappears.

Feb 1 Victor appt. w/ New Chair AND someone breaks into his house (besides me). Lucky timing....

...or was it?

Q: What if robbers knew he wasn't going 2 b in? --> Then the robbery must have been organized by someone who:

- knew Victor's schedule, Or
- knew the Chairman's schedule.
  ...including Victor or Chairman?????

Whaddya think?????

*

February 4, Early Morning
(Hour of the Angry E-mails)

Cathy—

You promised you would stay out of Victor's Biz. I'M NOT READING attached file. I'M NOT READING ANY MORE OF THIS. STOP IT.

Get your head back in the real world.

E

*

Emma—

Hello? Priorities? 4 some of us, high school isn't the whole of "the real world." We're not all getting in2 M.I.T.

4 God's sake, E—live a little. Break a rule sometime, just to see what it feels like. There's more 2 heaven & earth than Biz plans & good grades. Don't be the stereotype Nerdy asian Gradehound, @ least for an hour.

Need your help. Pls read.

Cathy

*

58

The instant I hit SEND I knew that one was a mistake. I shucked my PJs and got dressed for school with that sick feeling you get in your stomach when you know you just screwed up. On the plus side, it was time for Emma's bus to school. She probably wouldn't get the message until she got home.

I'd catch her at school, apologize in advance & tell her not to read the mail.

*

My computer pinged.

*

Cathy—

I'm the Suck. You're the Rebel. I'm about school. You're about Real Life. What's so funny is that you actually believe this.

OK, Cathy—here's some Real Life for you. In case you hadn't noticed, Cute High School Dropout w Fiery Temper doesn't pay very well in the Real World.

You're right—we aren't all going to M.I.T. For instance, our biology report was due yesterday, only you never did your part, did you? So much for my 4.0 GPA. Maybe I won't be getting into M.I.T. after all. Gee, thanks, best friend. What would I do without you?

Did you really listen to so much American radio you fell 4 the Teen Pop version of life? You think "U gotta fight 4 your right 2 PAAAAAR-TYYYYY!" is independence?

Independence isn't an ATTITUDE. Independence is a FACT. Independence is being able to make a car payment. Independence is not having to stay with a bf who beats you up because you can't pay for your own apartment.

Am I missing something, Cathy? Because after 8 months of nagging you to go to class, + helping you study for trig, + writing your entrance essay for Berkeley, it looks like the Cathy Life Plan is "Get a boyfriend who wants 2 support a Cute Artist." Is that really what your Dad would have wanted for you?

I guess you think it is. So, hey—maybe I'm wrong. Stalking a drug dealer so he'll take you back—maybe that IS a good long term play! Certainly better practice for the Real Life waiting for you than writing a stupid Biology paper.

59.

But I can't see myself helping out.

Sorry, Sorry, Sorry, Sorry, Sorry Sorry, Sorry, Sorry, Sorr

Emma (the Nerdy Asian Gradehound)

I phoned her but she wouldn't pick up. Then I threw my cell phone on the floor really hard and smashed it. It didn't make me feel any better.

One thing for sure: I was in no shape to go to school.

Feb 4, Afternoon
(Hour of the Rotten Ex-Best Friend)

Took a bus out to the mall, killing time. Read magazines in the Borders, looked at clothes. Took my sketch book but didn't feel like drawing. Scrounged free samples of Today's Baked Goods at Starbuck's until they started giving me the evil eye. Lunch was free samples at the Safeway: Soy Link Breakfast Sausage (yuck) and *Picante!* Brand Dips and Salsas (OK).

Independence is making a car payment. Pretty rich coming from a girl who plans to show she's a self-made woman by taking "only" a million dollars seed money from her Dad.

Anyway, I got "home from school" at the right time. Mom was already up. I waited for her to quiz me about homework. She didn't. I should have been relieved, but I wasn't. It doesn't feel like she trusts me, just like she's given up. Hey, join the club. New members every day.

She said Emma had called on the house phone. Whatever.

Feb 4, Afternoon
(Hour of the 17 consecutive games of Tetris on the computer)

… Enough moping. Obviously Emma's more interested in keeping her 4.0 than in figuring out why Victor was drugging me. There's some priorities for you. But whatever: as far as the mystery goes, I just have to work it out myself.

OK. Assume whoever robbed V's house knew he was going to be out— therefore, either had access to his schedule, or the Chairman's. "V steals from self" makes no sense. Therefore… New Chair (or someone in office) must be behind the robbery. Right?

62.

Why?

What did they know that I don't?

HEY! I think I've got it! What if ◁ — *I just cannot for the life of me remember what I figured out?*

Feb 4, Evening
(Hour of the Letter)

"Cathy!"

"What is it, Mom?"

"Someone to see you. He says it's about Victor."

My hands froze over my computer keyboard. My heart was racing. "Who is it?"

"Cathy!" Mom stuck her head into my bedroom. "Will you get out here, please?"

"Is it the cops?"

"Cops?" My mother looked at me sharply. "Why would it be the cops?"

I saved my file. I had a wild thought about sneaking out my window, but my Mom stayed right in the doorway, waiting for me. "Coming," I said.

*

The Prime Minister was sitting at our kitchen table. He didn't look like a Chinese Diplomat from the '20's anymore; today he looked like a HK business dude, with a nice Italian suit and shoes. Still had the diamond thing going on— the same diamond-shaped diamond cufflinks, and a diamond pattern on his silk tie. He could have been the Vice President of a computer company.

"Here she is," my mom said. "Would you like some coffee, Mr….?"

"Tsao." He tilted his head politely to me—the shadow of a bow. "Thank you, Mrs. Vickers. Do not trouble yourself."

"No trouble. I work a night shift, and I just made a pot." She was already dressed in her nurse uniform, with the heavy-duty support hose and thick-soled white shoes. She poured herself a cup of coffee, and rooted around in the refrigerator. With the fridge door between her and Mr. Tsao, she glanced up at me, raising her eyebrows questioningly. I gave a tiny shake of my head. She nodded. "I've got to head in to the hospital pretty soon," she said, smiling over her shoulder at Mr. Tsao. "I'm afraid you'll have to make this quick. I'm sure you understand."

Bless you, Mom.

61.

"Of course," Tsao said politely.

"How did you know where to find us?" I asked.

"Victor told me about you. I knew your last name and neighborhood. Your address I found in the phone book."

Mom sipped her coffee. "You're a regular detective."

"I have had some practice, trying to find my nephew."

Nephew? I took another look at Tsao. Maybe he was the mysterious uncle that Victor claimed was the real owner of the house in San Francisco, and the plane. Maybe Tsao was a wanted criminal, and that was why the house was in Victor's name….?

What if this "family affection" was really about Victor taking money that didn't belong to him, or failing to make a drug delivery, or refusing to do any more work on a new line of drugs?

My head was starting to spin.

"I take it Victor doesn't always want to be found," my mother said.

"Very true. He feels very alone. But that is exactly why he needs his family around him." Tsao's expression was grave. "You see, my nephew has a very serious, incurable medical condition."

Plus - if he was a crimina did that me I shouldn't help him fi Victor

My stomach lurched. "Victor! Victor was never sick a day in his life!"

"Victor is sick every day of his life," Tsao said. "When he was still a young man, he discovered that, as strong as he felt, he would never live to a normal age."

I couldn't believe it.

Tsao sighed. "Knowing such a thing changes a man. All he wants is to forget what he knows—to have the same simple dreams as everyone else. To find a wife, to marry, to work and raise children. And yet he knows the lie that would be. How can you marry, knowing that your body is a traitor that will force you to abandon your family? Knowing your children are doomed to lose their father?" He spoke quietly, but the sense of a profound and terrible loneliness haunted him. A solitary man in the cemetery: that's how I would paint him, I thought. The last soldier of a vanished company.

Mom sighed. "ALS?"

Tsao hesitated. "I do not know the English phrase."

"Amyotrophic lateral sclerosis. We call it Lou Gehrig's disease," Mom said sadly. "Poor Victor."

No, I wanted to say. I don't believe you. But suddenly so many things made sense. The way he would say things other people wouldn't say, or do things normal people wouldn't do, as if he didn't care about embarrassment, or risk. It would explain Giselle and Bianca, too. Was it Giselle who couldn't handle living with a condemned man? Or maybe she knew about his disease when they married, but the shadow of death lay over them all the time, poisoning things, until they agreed to split up. After this last year with Mom, I know how hard it is to live with someone who can't escape from sadness.

Or maybe it was Victor who had left Giselle, convinced that it was better for her that way. Better for little Bianca never to know her father, than to lose him at eight, or twelve.

I remembered the way Victor had looked at me, that first day, when I showed him the picture of himself at fifty-five. I thought he had been struck because I was showing him a vision of his future, but that hadn't been it at all, had it? I had been showing him a future he could never, ever have.

If Victor had ALS, or some similar degenerative disease, that would explain his decision to go into molecular biology in the first place. He wasn't in research to make a career—he was trying to *save his own life.*

Tsao slipped a folded sheet of paper out of the breast pocket of his suit jacket. "Victor preferred not to be a burden on his family, but we did correspond from time to time. He wrote very movingly about you." He handed me Victor's letter. "I do not know how you feel towards my nephew now. He has a habit of leaving suddenly. If you were angry, it would be only what he deserved. But perhaps now you understand him better. If you have any idea where he might have gone, I would be very grateful if you would contact me." Tsao thoughtfully rubbed his cheek where I had slapped him the day before. "You have a spirited daughter, Mrs. Vickers," he said, glancing at me with laughter in his eyes. "Out of curiosity, when was she born?"

"How old is she?" Mother looked at him, puzzled. "Just about to turn—"

"Oh my God, Mom—look at the time!" I blurted. "You're going to be late!"

Mom sighed and put down her coffee. "Yeah. I'm sorry, Mr. Tsao, but I have to go, and I'm not comfortable leaving you in the house with Cathy. I hope you understand."

"Of course." He rose, impeccably polite. "Do read the letter, Miss Vickers. I have enclosed a card. If you hear from Victor, I hope you will let me know."

*

When they had both left, I read Victor's letter. ~~Ten~~ times.

Oh, my God.

Feb 5, Morning
(Hour of the Depressed Detective)

Started to call Emma last night to read her V's letter, then remembered:

A)   She doesn't care & thinks I'm a stupid spoiled brat, &

B)   I smashed my cell phone.

Of course I could have used the house phone, but that's not the point. If she really thinks I'm just a spoiled whiny play-acting wannabe painter with no ambition higher than picking up abusive boyfriends, better to know now.

Oh, God. I screwed up her Biology paper. Damn, damn, damn.

Whole stupid fight makes me feel furious and hurt and ashamed and sick to my stomach.

I'm trying to mostly hang on to furious.

*

Anyway…

Not sure what to make of Tsao. I'm sure he was telling at least part of the truth. It just *fits*.

- There's something wrong with V, something medical…
- …That pushed him into research.

  This "problem,"—whatever it is—keeps him from forming long-term attachments with other people.

That explains why it always felt as if he liked me *in spite of himself*. (Kinda flattering.)

…And then he ditched me when things got hot. Which hurt: but compared to Giselle and Bianca, I've got no right to complain. I'm missing out on a guy I only knew for a couple of months, and never quite kissed. Giselle's missing a husband. Bianca's been abandoned by her Dad.

That's wrong.

64.

He was wrong to leave them. I know he's hurting, I know he's in trouble. I could forgive him for bailing on me. But leaving that little girl... that's harder to forgive. If I find him, I'm going to tell him that he has to get back in her life. He has to make it up to her.

As far as finding Victor goes, I can think of three obvious leads to follow:

1) Go back and search the house again. Not wild about this plan.

2) Check the airplane hangar. Isn't that where you would leave useful stuff if you were planning to make a quick getaway? Even if the plane was gone, that would tell you something, wouldn't it?

3) Go to Intrepid Biotech (now a wholly-owned subsidiary of P'eng-Lai Pharmaceuticals, I guess) and see what might be lying around on his desk.

*

Hey, wait a minute

Assume for a second V was filching lab time & resources to work on a project related to his illness and Carla found out about it.

That still doesn't explain why she should end up dead. It wasn't like she surprised him and he hit her and accidentally killed her. This was multiple gunshots to the stomach. That's cold-blooded murder, and you don't do that because you've been working on a few experiments after hours. There's not enough at stake.

Unless....

Unless Victor found a *cure*????? A cure for ALS? He might kill to protect *that,* right? If he felt his life was on the line, and the lives of thousands of others with his disease.

Q: So for $64,000 dollars and a shrink-wrapped edition of our Home Game, *what did Victor stick in my arm?*

A: You know what would really suck? *If he thought he had a cure, and infected me with the disease, to see if it would work.*

????

*

Just went on the web and researched Lou Gehrig's disease.

Oh, my God.

*

Too freaked out to think straight.

I'm going to go to school and have a really normal day and not think about anything, anything, anything.

Oh, my god.

Feb 5, Afternoon
(Hour of June at the Reception Desk)

Hey, I *did* go to school.

I just didn't *stay* there.

I hung in for two whole classes before cutting out during P.E. We were doing Lacrosse. I waited until Ms. Greep was on the other side of the field and pretended my ball had gone into the street. Climbed the fence in my gym shorts and jogged all the way home. That's a workout, right?

I made up a story about having forgotten my homework in case Mom woke up while I was in the house, but she was zonked on her usual combination of depression, exhaustion, and Gordon's Extra Dry Gin.

Machine was blinking by the phone. Message from Emma. I erased it.

OK. First up: airplane hangar, followed by Intrepid Biotech.

Can't really go in default Artist Chic. ArtGirl jumps into her closet…

… and comes out Transformed! Behold my Secret Identity: Respectable DroneGrrl!

- Black skirt—the one I wore to Daddy's funeral.
- Pantyhose. The only pair I could find had several runs, but I remembered the old trick about locking them with nail polish, which was good. My only nail polish = Eggplant Purple, which was bad. I locked all the runs I guessed would be below the hemline. Better be ladylike when crossing my legs, though; anyone peeking under my skirt is going to wonder how I got purple fingerprints all over my thighs.
- White stretch shirt—the one with the gorgeous appliqué Minotaur on back.
- Navy jacket—from Freshman Choir. Jacket can't be buttoned across my front anymore (ahem), but its main job is to cover up

66.

Waterproof Mascara
— "Very Black"

CoverGirl Lipgloss
"Demure"

White
Shirt

navy
Jacket

black
skirt.

Respectable Drone Girrrl

Sneakers
(opted for function
over form!!)

67.

the leering Minotaur (see shirt, above). Sleeves are a bit short, but who notices sleeves, anyway?

- Shoes—always a problem. Alternatives:
    - White sneakers (too informal. Also, muddy from jog home)
    - Strappy sandals (too slutty)
    - leather boots (get real)
    - pumps (still can't walk in heels. Since object of exercise is Blending In, falling off my shoes to land on butt, exposing Purple Fingerprints (see Pantyhose, above) not such a good idea.

  And the winner is: sneakers.

Best Part: since mom is still home, I can actually Drive the Car!!!!! Wish me luck.

Feb 5, Evening
(Hour of the DroneGrrl)

Some Break & Enters are easier than others.

1. Victor's house: so easy I didn't even know I was doing it.
2. The hangar where he kept his airplane: a piece of cake. He hadn't bothered to close the padlock on the door; it was just hanging there for decorative effect. Couldn't find much of interest inside, except a little gray metal filing cabinet. Inside it was all just airplane stuff—maintenance logs, license requirements, and about a zillion maps. Nothing I was smart enough to recognize as a smoking gun. The only weird thing was a little folder marked LAFAYETTE ESCADRILLE, with a bunch of old stuff in it. I didn't want to hang around long enough for an airport employee to ask me what the heck I was doing there without Victor, so I just stuck the folder in my backpack and sauntered back to Mom's car. I'll go through the stuff later tonight.

Assuming my hands ever stop shaking, and the cops don't have me in custody, that is…. Which brings us to…

3. Intrepid Biotech, *"Making Tomorrow—Today!"* ™

Intrepid was headquartered in a typical Silicon Valley business park on the outskirts of San Jose. Rooflines were low. Glass was plentiful. Cars were foreign.

My Cunning Plan was to sneak into Victor's office and see if I could turn up any clues as to where he had gone, or what he had been working on. I was kinda nervous. Of course, my first two B&E's had gone off very smoothly. Probably I'm just damn good at this life of crime stuff, I told myself. Either that, or disaster was already overdue.

I pulled on the tiller of Mom's land-yacht ("pre-owned" white '91 Mercury Marquis with red velour upholstery) and turned it into the parking lot, where I docked it between a Volvo station wagon and a BMW with a Garfield sucker doll clamped to the back window. I sort of dinged the Beamer when I opened my door, but I spat on my finger and rubbed at the scratch until you could hardly tell.

As I glanced around to see if anyone had noticed me working on the BMW's paint job, a beat-up Chevette came rocketing into the lot, bucked over the speed bump at the turn, and jerked to a stop at the first available space. A frantic red-head in a bad beige suit squeezed out clutching a file folder, and hurried toward the Intrepid building. Hey, I thought—someone more rattled than me! ☺
I followed the red-head into the lobby, which was decorated in Modern Corporate Bland (Stained Pine and Steel division). I guess she must have been expecting the inner doors to open automatically, because when they didn't, she hit 'em like a sparrow smacking into a kitchen window. She reeled around a bit, clutching her nose, while a sheaf of paper fountained out of her manila folder and spilled to the floor.

The waiting area featured a long counter to one side, like a hotel front desk. A professional-looking receptionist sat behind it, armed with one of those thin headset phones, a winning smile, and a set of visitor badges. Her name tag said JUNE R. Getting by her was the only way into the rest of Intrepid, and the inner set of glass doors could only be opened by swiping with a pass key. June R. rose from behind the counter and did a worried face at the woman kneeling woozily on the floor. "Ma'am?"

HELLO my name is

I'm making tommorrow today!

JUNE. R

"Oh, God, I feel like such an idiot!" Ol' Sparky was still holding her nose as if she had just stuck it back on after a nasty accident and had to wait a few minutes for the glue to dry. "I'm already late, and I was thinking—I'm sorry, I guess I have to sign in or something, I'm here to see Joe Schmidt, I'm his 12:30, only my regular sitter phoned this morning to say she couldn't take Kasey because she had mono, the sitter that is, not Kasey, Kasey gets ear infections sometimes, but never mono." The red-head was scrabbling around on the floor for her spilled papers. "—So I had to *beg* my neighbors to take her for the day and I couldn't get out of the house, and then the *car* wouldn't—"

"Don't worry about it," June said quickly. "Mr. Schmidt is running a little behind schedule anyway. His twelve o'clock hasn't come out yet. As far as he knows, you were here right on time." She consulted a clip-board on her desk. "Job interview for Mary Gantry? Come sign in, and I'll buzz Joe."

Still on all fours in the Intrepid lobby, Mary Gantry looked up like a grateful red-headed calf. "Thank you so much," she said thickly.

June and I both looked away, in case she needed to cry.

The receptionist punched a number into her switchboard. "Mr. Schmidt? I have your 12:30 still waiting in the lobby here, and we were just wondering how much longer— Unh-hunh?" She grinned at Mary Gantry and held a conspiratorial finger over her lips. "Unh-hunh. Okay, then. I'll let her know."

I decided I liked June.

She passed a clipboard across the counter. "When you're done signing in, you need to give me a Visitor Parking Form," she said, pointing at a tray of pink slips. I picked one up and started to fill it out, buying time to think.

Mary Gantry and I were standing shoulder to shoulder. I snuck a glance at the clipboard. There were two listed appointments for 1:00, Jim Ellis and Peter de Vries. My heart sank. The next woman listed was Bernice Lau, due at 1:30. Mary signed her name and then waffled over "Time In". June glanced up at the lobby clock, which said 12:42, and gave Mary a conspiratorial smile. She wrote a shaky 12:30 in the box.

"Mr. Schmidt will be down for you in just a minute," June said.

Oh, great. She wasn't even going to give us badges and buzz us in. Apparently, visitors had to be personally escorted inside the premises.

check the box which applies:

1. Are you an idiot?

☑ *yes*   ☐ *no*

Time to give up. That would be the smart play. That's what Emma would do.

June took back her clipboard and turned to me. "May I help you?"

"I'm here to see Mr. Schmidt." *What was I doing!* "I-I think I'm early."

June looked doubtfull at her clipboard. "Bernice Lau?"

"It's Swiss," I said. "Not the Chinese Lau. Lau as in 'Lausanne.'" I was pretty sure there was something named Lausanne in either France or Switzerland. A town, or a kind of cow, or something.

"I never knew Lau was a Swiss name!" June said brightly.

"Most people don't."

June's eyes skipped over my too-tight navy jacket with the too-short sleeves. Her smile got wider and more sympathetic. "I'm afraid Mr. Schmidt is running a little behind," she said. "You'll have to wait in the lobby."

I printed BERNICE LAU above my license plate number on the pink Visitor Parking form.

Inside the building, a set of elevator doors opened and spat out a harassed-looking guy with a comb-over. "Do you have a cafeteria?" I asked, thinking fast. "Or a vending machine? I didn't have a chance to get lunch." I bent my ArtGrrl mental powers on June, willing her to ask Joe to let me into the building along with Mary.

"I'm sorry," June said, like she really truly was, "but I'm afraid we can't do that."

Rats.

Joe Schmidt collected the hapless Mary Gantry and chaperoned her into Intrepid with a swish of his passkey, leaving me out in the lobby.

I paced.

June watched me. "I have some gum, if that would help," she said, digging in her purse and pulling out a stick of Freedent. "It's sugarless."

It was icy mint flavor. Not bad.

I sat down in a comfy chair and pretended to read a copy of the Wall Street Journal. The way I figured it, I ought to have at least half an hour before Bernice Lau showed up. On the other hand, I was fresh out of ideas. There was information I really, really needed, just on the other side of those glass doors. At the very least I might get another clue or two about Victor, or the late lamented

71.

Carla Beckman. (I'm sorry for every nasty thought I had about you, Carla!)

In the worst case scenario, I had been infected with some kind of horrible disease, and the only way I was going to find a cure was to track down Victor, or discover an antidote stashed somewhere in his lab. I sighed and swore under my breath.

"Are you feeling okay, Bernice?"

I looked up and found June looking back at me, even more sympathetically. My spidey-sense tingled, letting me know my skirt had ridden up a couple of inches in the comfy chair and she had seen the eggplant-colored fingerprints on my ratty pair of nylons.

"Is there a bathroom?" I said faintly.

"Just to your left, dear."

I went into the john and locked the door. I took off my navy jacket and my white blouse so they wouldn't get wet, then took four big fistfuls of paper towels from the dispenser over the sink. I jammed them into the bottom of the toilet until I was satisfied that it was completely blocked. Then I flushed. Several times.

When water was running nicely all over the bathroom floor, I patted my arm dry, shrugged into my blouse, and put the navy jacket back on.

I stuck my head out of the door. "Hey—the toilet's out of order."

June did a frown. "Let me take a look." She stepped out from behind her counter and opened the bathroom door, then made a sort of squeak as water lapped softly against her Naturalizers. "I see what you mean."

"Geez, I don't mean to be a bother," I said, "but I'm really feeling sick, um, down there."

*

Two minutes later I was alone in the cafeteria bathroom. June was on her headset, talking to maintenance. I had promised her I would wait in the cafeteria for Joe Schmidt.

This was a lie.

A real Fearless Lady Detective would probably be feeling pretty cocky after having wormed her way through security, but in truth I was somewhere between "dithery" and "panic-stricken". I was now in a secured building under false pretenses, and I got the feeling that Intrepid would press charges of Criminal Trespass if I got caught. Plus, it was almost one o'clock—it wouldn't be long

72.

before the real Bernice Lau showed up, and the fun would start in earnest.

I had no idea where Victor's lab was. Or if he had an office separate from the lab. Or where he would have kept his stuff.

I scanned the cafeteria, looking for a mid-level manager. I wanted a guy, someone who wouldn't notice the defects in my wardrobe; the sort who offers you a seat on the bus if you smile the right way. I picked him out three tables away, a roly-poly gentleman in his early forties, weak chin hidden under a slightly graying beard (good choice—his wife was looking after him) nice shirt and tie. He was sitting by himself, working his way through a slice of pecan pie.

"Hi," I said. "Um, can I ask you a question?"

Pecan Pie paused, fork in the air. "Yes?"

"I was supposed to meet someone here, Victor Chan? He was going to talk to me about interning…?" It was no trouble pretending to be nervous. "I think maybe we got our wires crossed. He said his office number, but I thought we were supposed to meet here, and I've forgotten it. Is there, like, an office directory or something?"

Pecan Pie frowned thoughtfully. He reached over to the next table and tapped on the wrist of a young woman drinking a soy latte. "Victor Chan," he said. "Works in the Alphabet, right?"

"Lab C?" Soy Latte said. "Or D. I'm in B," she said with a friendly smile. "She's looking for Victor?"

"Thinking of interning," Pecan Pie said.

Soy Latte's eyebrows rose. "Now? With all the reorg?"

"Maybe I was too slow," I said, backpedaling. "I knew Victor from school."

"Another one!" Pecan Pie said, astonished. "All these kids going to the Sorbonne! What's wrong with good old Cal?"

The *Sorbonne*???? As in, *Paris*????

"Try the Alphabet," Pecan Pie said. "Second floor labs, down the corridor to the right. I'm thinking Lab C."

"Or D," Soy Latte said.

"Got it." I fled.

*

73.

I went completely frantic trying to find Victor's freaking lab. Minutes flew at me like bullets, each one closer: 1:10, 1:11, 1:12… He didn't even have an office, as it turned out—just a lab bench with a desk at the end of it. I would have walked right past Victor's space in Lab A (curse you, Soy Latte!) if I hadn't noticed a little cork message board with one of my drawings thumb-tacked to it. It was a self-portrait he had asked me for—myself, exactly my real age. In the midst of my panic, I had a brief, knee-buckling moment of tenderness, seeing it there.

The rest of the lab was empty, thank God. Not totally surprising—it was still lunch time, almost, and of course Victor was missing. Carla Beckman, who should have been working at the next bench over, had taken the week off with a bad case of death.

I stared at the cork board, trying to figure out what I should be looking for. 1:17, 1:18. At any moment Bernice Lau would be showing up in the lobby, if she wasn't there already. For all I knew, company security was already hustling to Joe Schmidt's office.

Victor's lab book—plain, black, hardcover, not so different from my sketchbook—was lying on the counter underneath the message board. I flipped it open. Nothing, of course. Victor would keep notes on his secret work somewhere else. But if there was another, secret lab book, I couldn't find it...

The rest of the bench was clean. The drawers in the desk at the end of it were locked.

1:20

Helpful June was probably doing a frown at the real Bernice Lau right at this moment.

I hurried over to Carla's bench and tried her desk drawers. Also locked.

Footsteps came echoing down the corridor outside. I dropped to a crouch, hiding behind Carla's desk, breathing as quietly as possible. My eye fell on a couple of pieces of paper that had slipped down between the desk and the cubicle divider.

I froze as the footsteps paused at the door to Lab A…. and then passed slowly down the corridor.

Whew.

I plucked the sheets of paper from behind the desk. They were Xerox copies of some kind of scientific measurement, and they had notes on them in Victor's handwriting.

Carla had found the secret notebook! I felt it, sure as my own racing heartbeat. She had found some of Victor's results and photocopied them. Hands shaking, I stuffed the copies into my purse and ran to the lab door.

1:26

Eek! Portrait!

Slapping my hand to my forehead, I raced back and ripped my picture off Victor's cork board. Couldn't have the cops showing that to June R., or Pecan Pie.

1:28

I couldn't risk going out the front door, I would have to follow the exit signs and run out a back way, then get to my car—

My car! I had a nightmare vision of Bernice Lau at the front desk while June capably went through the visitor parking forms, and I was going to be so busted, because like a freaking idiot *I had written down my real license plate number.*

I followed an EXIT sign to a set of stairs and went hammering down them, three at a time, noise booming in the concrete stairwell. I burst out a side door on the ground floor and pelted into the parking lot, hunched over so as to keep a line of cars between me and the front door. I found the Mercury and slid in from the passenger side. It took me three tries to get the key in my trembling hands to fit into the ignition. In the rear-view mirror I saw two rent-a-cops in blue uniforms emerging from the Intrepid lobby. They started to run towards me. I screeched backward out of my parking space, got the Mercury's nose pointed for the exit, and hit the gas.

75

- Cover Girl
  Liquid Pencil Eyeliner

- Eye Shadow "Shimmering Onyx"

- Lipgloss — "Edgy"

- Waterproof Mascara
  — "Very Black."

Part III
February 5, Evening Still
(Hour of the GothGrrl)

I was glad my Drivers Ed. teacher wasn't in the car on the way home. First, I would have failed the class, and second, I would have had to wipe off my mom's upholstery where he messed his pants. I wondered if Intrepid had called the cops. They might be on the phone to the DMV *right now,* running Mom's license plate number, because I was stupid enough to write it on the parking permission slip. There might be a black and white waiting in our driveway *by the time I got home.*

Some jerk in a Volvo station wagon blasted his horn at me just because I was driving in two lanes at once. I scowled at the driver and tried shooting lightning bolts out my eyes at him, on the off-chance Victor had injected me with a top-secret serum to turn me into a mutant superhero named HellCath who would wear black Levis with sharpened buttons and a severe spandex tuxedo and haunt the BART stations at night on the watch for evil-doers.

No lightning bolts. Rats.

I parked three blocks from my house so I could make sure there weren't cops there waiting for me. I sat at the curb hyperventilating for a while and then changed into another one of my Impenetrable Disguises. The dressy black skirt was a bit of a problem. Since I didn't keep a spare pair of pants in my glove compartment, like Easy Sally Thurston, I had to work towards the black skirt, instead of away from it. I Gothed out my eyes with gobs of eye-shadow, and used some drawing ink as emergency black nail polish. I shucked the navy choir blazer and turned my shirt around so the lurid Minotaur painting was face front. Then I dug around in the Mercury's upholstery until I found a couple of hair ties and did some of those stubby little Bjork pigtails that stand up from the top of your head like sea anemone tentacles. I inspected the final product in the mirror, hoping there wasn't much resemblance to the fake Bernice Lau who had presented herself at Intrepid two hours before. I thought about using a lipstick to give myself some fake zits, but they didn't look very convincing, and anyway I didn't want everyone in my neighborhood thinking my skin was gross.

I did a quick perv check to make sure the sidewalks were empty, then sunk down in the front seat and wiggled out of my pantyhose. I balled them up inside the navy jacket, got out of the car, and stuffed the whole wad down the mouth of a storm sewer by the car. Good nesting material for whatever lived down there. Raccoons. Crocodiles.

Okay. Time to saunter by the house and see who had it staked out.

*

And the winner was: Emma.

*

Flip-flop, my stomach said. No way should the sight of Emma stalking up and down the sidewalk in front of my house be scarier than the police, but my stomach didn't seem to understand that. Flip-flop. Flip-flop.

Stupid stomach.

Emma had always been there for me, through all the back-stabbing Popular Girls of Junior High, through my run of spectacularly bad boyfriends—the grabby one who wouldn't wash, the shy one who couldn't kiss, the mean one whose car I set on fire—through hours of tutoring in algebra and chemistry, paid for with sketches and comics and gossip and pizza, she had always been there.

I could still remember the dress she wore to my Dad's funeral—black rayon, mid-calf, serious, surprisingly grown up. Emma hadn't bought anything for Junior High Prom or her first High School dance, but she'd gone out on her own to buy that dress.

My eyes ached and I was afraid I was going to cry.

Crossing the street to my house was like forcing myself to put my hand down on a burner. I thought of how I must look, with my Goth eye make-up and my shirt on backwards. My cheeks began to burn. Thank god I hadn't painted extra zits on my face.

Emma saw me. "Cathy! Good grief, you look like the victim at the beginning of a Buffy episode."

And what I wanted to say was, Oh God, I'm so sorry about the Biology paper, I never meant to let you down. But what came out of my mouth was, "Have you been waiting long?"

"Yeah," she said. "Look, I brought you a cell phone. I figured maybe yours was broken," she said. "And then you weren't checking your machine." She handed over a phone the size of a ladies' electric razor, with buttons and screens so high-tech and rounded and slanting it had probably been crafted by hyper-intelligent captive dolphins with electrodes implanted directly into their brains, down which streamed an endless collage of Danish Modern design magazines. "Don't worry, it was way cheaper in Hong Kong, no big deal and I've got lots better now. It has a radio built in," she said. Silence gathered. "Also a flashlight," she said.

"I don't think I ought to take—"

"This way," Emma hurried on, "if something really important happens, I can call you, like this." She took out a second phone barely as big as her thumb and snapped it open like a switchblade. "Call Cathy," she said, and three seconds later, the dolphin phone in my hand played the opening two bars of the Verve's "Bittersweet Symphony" in FM quality sound, which I guess is what phones do when they're too cool to just, you know, ring.

"Shouldn't you be in class?" I said.

"Answer your phone."

"Emma, I'm standing right—"

"Go ahead. Answer it. I want to make sure it works, in case there's an emergency."

I rolled my eyes and pressed the Talk button. "Hello?"

"WELL GUESS WHO DECIDED TO FINALLY ANSWER HER DAMN PHONE!" Emma shouted, loud enough to make my eardrums throb. I jerked the dolphin phone from my ear and held it at arm's length.

Emma was shaking with fury. "I realize you have your little issues with the drug-dealer and everything, but right now my entire life has just turned to crap, and I appear to be such a loser that you, despite being a self-centered ditz who exploits me at every turn, are the only best friend I've got." Emma paused to catch her breath, still glaring into her cell phone instead of looking at me. "So you're going to stop whining about your own problems. You are going to STAND THERE and BE NICE TO ME or I am going to PUNCH YOU IN THE FACE."

"That seems fair," I said. But what I was thinking was, *She forgives me!*

Emma glowered at her phone as if it were a small silver bug she was dying to crush in her fist. "My Dad's at home," she said. "In my apartment. He slept on my couch last night."

"I didn't know he was coming for a visit."

79.

"It's not a visit. He's moving in."

"What?"

She squatted down on the porch step and stared out at my street, bleak-eyed. "It's all gone. The dealership. The holding company. The stores. The website. The apartment in Hong Kong. The house on Macao. Everything. He's not sleeping on my couch because he dropped in for a visit. He's sleeping on my couch because he has nowhere else to stay. He's ruined. We're ruined."

"But what about your company? What about your one million dollars of seed money? What about M.I.T.?"

She scowled and spoke loudly into her cell phone. **"There is no seed money**. There is no money for M.I.T. unless I pull a scholarship."

I felt the blood drain from my face. I had cost Emma her A in biology. Suddenly she needed a scholarship to get into college, and I had cost her an A.

Her eyes were distant. "I think it got so bad because he was scared to tell me. He let it go on, and on, hoping he would get lucky, hoping something would turn around. But it didn't. And now we don't have anything."

"What about the apartment?" I said weakly.

"It's on a six-month lease that comes up in three weeks. We're going to have to get a cheaper place. Dad says this is just a temporary setback. He's been on the phone non-stop since he got in." Her face crumpled up. "Long distance calls, Cathy! Long distance to Taipei and HK and Shenzen! How are we going to pay for that?"

"He can get a job."

"Him? Oh, no. He doesn't have jobs," she said bitterly. "He has schemes. Schemes are much less boring than jobs. I'm the one who'll have to get a job." She snapped the cell phone shut and stuck it into her backpack. "You were right," she said. "You were absolutely right. I was so arrogant. There I was, thinking I was queen of the freaking universe. Everything all planned out." She turned to look at me, and her mouth trembled. "Oh, Cathy ... I already bought shelf-paper for my apartment in Boston."

I put my arm around her shoulders. "Shhhhhh, sweetie."

Her eyes squinched shut. "I already bought my s-shelf p-p-p-p-aper," she sobbed. "Three days ago I had a *dream*, Cathy. I had *goals*." She hiccupped a sad

80.

hiccup. "Now I'm no better off than *you!*"

I accidentally dug my comforting fingernails into her arm.

"I have a new plan," Emma announced.

"Yeah?"

"We've got to find Victor."

I blinked. "Victor the low-down double-crossing drug dealer?"

"But he's rich," Emma said. "It's always important to cultivate acquaintances of high net worth."

"Emma!"

"There's no upside dealing with *poor* double-crossing drug dealers," Emma said reasonably.

"Ah. Good point. You are joking, right?"

"The 30/30 plan is in serious danger," Emma said. "The situation calls for desperate measures."

"You want to find Victor, seduce him, and wheedle a million bucks out of him."

"I thought you could do the seducing. You're cuter," she said morosely.

"You must really not want to be poor," I said.

"Broke artists are glamorous," Emma said. "A broke businesswoman is just pathetic."

*

Feb 6, Very Awfully Darn Late
(Hour of the Instant Messenger)

—IM log from bizarre and eye-popping conversation…

*

Emma says: (11:41:32 PM)
     Got it!!!!

Cathy says: (11:41:42 PM)
        ?

Emma says: (11:41:50 PM)
    I've been plowing thru cancer
    research online and I have some
    ideas about what Victor was doing.

Cathy says: (11:41:57 PM)
      !

Emma says: (11:42:15 PM)
    TRAP assays!
    TRAP = Telomere Repeats
    Amplification Protocol

Cathy says: (11:42:26 PM)
    Oh! NOW I get it!
    </Fe>

Emma says: (11:42:32 PM)
    Check the attached page
    <incoming>

    telomeres = bits of cell that get
    shorter every time cell divides.
    Think shoelaces; each new pair of
    shoes, U cut laces in half 2 lace up
    new pair, OK? After N new pairs,
    laces 2 short 2 tie any more —>
    No more new shoes.

Cathy says: (11:43:17 PM)
    What's wrong w/cells just dividing
    4ever?

Emma says: (11:43:34 PM)
        = cancer

Cathy says: (11:43:41 PM)
☹

Cathy says: (11:43:58 PM)
OK, I'm looking @ the notes w/yr stickies. Keep talking, bt use small words. Better yet, skip 2 the end & tell me what u think it means....

Yes, Miss Cheung.
No, Miss Cheung.

Emma says: (11:44:36 PM)
you could at least try 2 figure it out, 2 make up 4 blowing off our paper....

Victor Says: (11:44:40 PM)
STAY AWAY FROM INTREPID!

Cathy says: (11:44:47 PM)
EMMA!

Cathy Says: (11:44:48 PM)
Victor! LTNC!

Where are you?

Emma says: (11:44:56 PM)
CATHY! ... wassup?

Victor Says: (11:45:13 PM)
What the hell did you think you were playing at, Cathy?

Emma says: (11:45:13 PM)
ANYWAY, V could B just researching another cancerous cell line ... but why would anyone get shot ovr that? IMHO, V's project = slowing down cellular aging.

Victor Says: (11:45:17 PM)
Cathy? This is important.

Cathy Says: (11:45:25 PM)
Ur IM = "appear offline" I never would have known you were OL, cept you pinged me. You pinged cuz you want 2 talk w/ me.

Emma says: (11:45:28 PM)
NOTE: cellular aging isn't the same as ORGANISM aging. 2 keep a whole PERSON from getting old, you need 2 solve a whole bunch of other problems—free radical oxidation, etc.

Victor Says: (11:45:32 PM)
Because you're driving me crazy!

Cathy Says: (11:45:40 PM)
+ you wanted 2 talk 2 me. You miss me. Cathy & Victor, sitting in a tree—

Emma says: (11:45:42 PM)
But even slowing cell age would = big $. E.g. cosmetics — how about wrinkle cream *that really works*? How much $ would 47 yo woman pay 2 have 17 yo skin?

Cathy says: (11:45:45 PM)
K – I – S – S – I – N – G!

Cathy says: (11:46:06 PM)
V just pinged me!

Victor Says: (11:46:10 PM)
Why did you go to my office?!?

Emma says: (11:46:12 PM)
!!!!!!!!!!!!

Emma says: (11:46:16 PM)
What's happening?

Cathy says: (11:46:28 PM)
I'm baiting him, & he's yelling @ me for going 2 Intrepid.

Emma says: (11:46:39 PM)
LOL! I like him better now.

Emma says: (11:46:45 PM)
FWIW—tell him I have a great place 2 launder drug $. For the low price of 1 of those floating goat paintings you like so much, I have a once-n-a-lifetime opportunity! Get in on the ground floor of 2xTalk Wireless Co., the next telecom giant!!!!!

Cathy says: (11:46:57 PM)
:-/

Emma says: (11:47:15 PM)
Hey—if he knows you went to Intrepid, HE MUST BE STALKING YOU, TOO!
How romantic!

Cathy says: (11:47:22 PM)
:-/?
He says he got his $ on the stock market.

Emma says: (11:47:32PM)
YSR.

Cathy says: (11:47:35PM)
Ever hear of a guy named George Wingfield?

Emma says: (11:47:46 PM)
No.

?

Cathy says: (11:47:54 PM)
He says he killed Carla!

Cathy Says: (11:46:14 PM)
How did U know I went there?

Victor Says: (11:46:19 PM)
A little bird told me.

Cathy Says: (11:46:32 PM)
Emma thinks you're making drugs.

Victor Says: (11:46:39 PM)
She's wrong.

Cathy Says: (11:46:46 PM)
YSR.

So where does all the $$$ come from?

Victor Says: (11:46:55 PM)
Stocks. Mines, mostly. Some banks. I had a friend, a good friend who gave me some good advice.

Cathy Says: (11:47:09 PM)
What friend?

Victor Says: (11:47:22 PM)
George Wingfield.

Stay out of my business, Cathy. You don't want to end up like Carla, do you?

Cathy Says: (11:47:29 PM)
Who killed her?

Victor Says: (11:47:32 PM)
Me.

Cathy Says: (11:47:36 PM)
You're just saying that.

Victor Says: (11:47:43PM)
You wanted me to answer questions. I'm answering questions.

left har man

sort o

true

86

Emma says: (11:48:02 PM)
Why?

Cathy says: (11:48:08 PM)
<asking>

Emma says: (11:48:15 PM)
We know he was working on something @ the lab. Something —> anti-aging

Cathy says: (11:48:27 PM)

OMG.
Just thought of something. Did U say he was measuring something between the 2 cancers?

Emma says: (11:48:37 PM)
Yeah

Cathy says: (11:48:48 PM)
Victor's dying. Could it B cancer?

Emma says: (11:48:55 PM)
! Dying!!!!!!!
????

Cathy says: (11:49:08 PM)
His uncle told me. = why he left Giselle & Bianca. Diagnosd w/ ALS or something like it.

Cathy says: (11:49:16 PM)
Secret project = cure 4 cancer?????

—> would = huge $$$$$$$$.

Emma says: (11:49:25 PM)
Hrm ... I don't *think* so. JM2C— science doesn't work like that (1 man = cure 4 cancer) cept in moviez. Even (1 man = great new wrinkle cream) is a stretch.

Might have cancer, tho. ☹

Another possible, w/ a cell age twist...

Cathy Says: (11:47:52PM)
I don't believe you. Why would you kill her?

Victor Says: (11:47:59PM)
Women around me have a bad habit of turning up dead, Cathy.

Cathy says: (11:48:06PM)
You're trying 2 scare me.

Victor Says: (11:48:14PM)
I can try harder.

Cathy Says: (11:48:20PM)
I think you're running away from me like U did from Giselle & Bianca.

Victor Says: (11:48:32PM)
You know they're dead too.

Cathy Says: (11:48:36PM)
Stop it. That's not funny.

Victor Says: (11:48:42PM)
No, it's not.
You really don't want to think I'm such a bad guy, do you? It's such a teenage girl thing. Cute, really, in a dumb way.

Look, I'll swear on a stack of Bibles, a crate of Korans: I kill people. I kill people and I don't even care. I've done it for sport. Only three or four times: it was a phase I was going through.

But if you stay around me long enough, you'll end up dead too. That's just what happens.

Cathy Says: (11:49:26 PM)
If you're such a monster, you wouldn't warn me. You'd have killed me already.

www.eurekalert.org/pub_releases/2003-01/mscc-mid0106 03.php

Dyskeratosis Congenita — premature aging. Possible?

MAKE COSMETICS NOT WAR

Cathy says: (11:49:48 PM)
He doesn't look old.

Emma says: (11:49:53 PM)
True. Rats.

Hey—Next Q: Who is "C"? That last entry in table: different subject, it looks like. Normal adult telomerase readings (i.e. basically zip)

Cathy says: (11:50:13 PM)
So the Minister turned out 2 B V's uncle, Tsao—but now V's saying he doesn't HAVE an uncle.
<eyeroll>
The letter about me—which I read—apparently doesn't exist.

Emma says: (11:50:22 PM)
Maybe V's right. Maybe U got conned. Maybe letter = fake & the "Uncle" guy forged it.

Cathy says: (11:50:36 PM)
No. I met him. He looked like V. Anyway, if the letter was fake, how would Tsao have found me? I never even told him my name.

Emma says: (11:50:45 PM)
CMIIW, but U wrote a check for the hell $, yeah?

Cathy says: (11:50:52 PM)
OMG

Emma says: (11:51:01 PM)
So yr name, address, & # would be

Cathy Says: (11:49:32 PM)
I know you're sick. I've talkd 2 yr uncle. He's looking for you. He wants 2 help U.

Victor Says: (11:49:36 PM)
I don't HAVE an uncle!!!!!!

Cathy Says: (11:49:42 PM)
You're lying like a rug.

Cathy Says: (11:49:47 PM)
He looks just like U. He's the 1 who gave U that jade pendant. Has 1 just like it, but bigger. V, stop lying 2 me.

Cathy Says: (11:49:52 PM)
You should talk 2 him. I don't know what kind of trouble you're in, but there's people who want 2 help. Trust me. Trust yr uncle.

Victor Says: (11:50:10 PM)
You sure he looks like *me*? We all look alike, you know.

Cathy Says: (11:50:13 PM)
HEY! This is ME, not other people. I may B White Kid From The Burbs, but Faces R Us, remember?

Victor Says: (11:50:20 PM)
—He says he gave me my jade pendant?

Cathy Says: (11:50:25 PM)
Yeah.

Victor Says: (11:50:32 PM)
I want to meet him.

Cathy Says: (11:50:40 PM)
Yr uncle?

Victor Says: (11:50:44 PM)
Right.

printed right on top for anyone 2 read, right?

Cathy says: (11:51:13 PM)
I thought you said you wouldn't read the stuff I sent about my trip to C-town?

Emma says: (11:51:25 PM)
Of COURSE I read it!

Cathy says: (11:51:38 PM)
Have I mentioned I hate U? Anyway, now he DOES have an uncle after all. Wants 2 meet him.

Emma says: (11:51:46 PM)
Meet his own uncle? Doesn't the uncle own the fancy house you burgled?

Cathy says: (11:51:54 PM)
He sez no.

Emma says: (11:52:02 PM)
He's lying.

Cathy Says: (11:52:16 PM)
Right. & I shouldn't give up Tsao's # —> – it's the only thing I have V wants.

Emma says: (11:52:27 PM)
HEY!!!!!!!!!! C = Cathy or Carla!!!!

Cathy! Ask him what happened 2 yr arm, Cathy! ASK HIM IF HE TOOK A BLOOD SAMPLE FROM YR ARM!

Cathy says: (11:52:41 PM)
—My "spider bite"! I got that needle mark right @ the end of January!

Cathy says: (11:52:56 PM)
But WHY?

Cathy Says: (11:50:49 PM)
I thought U didn't have an uncle.

Victor Says: (11:51:00 PM)
Sure I do. I just forgot. Did he give you an address, or #?

Cathy Says: (11:51:11 PM)
So this isn't the uncle who owns the house?

Victor Says: (11:51:19 PM)
No.

Cathy Says: (11:51:26 PM)
Different uncle.

Victor Says: (11:51:40 PM)
Right.
#s?

Cathy Says: (11:51:45 PM)
I don't have it right here.

Victor Says: (11:51:52 PM)
Don't screw around with me, Cathy. Carla did that, and look what happened to her.

Cathy Says: (11:52:05 PM)
I'll set up a F2F

Tell me when & where. I'll get word back 2 Tsao.

Victor Says: (11:52:27 PM)
11:00 AM Friday, at the Musee Mecanique. I don't want YOU there. I mean it, Cathy—if I spot you, the meeting is off.

Cathy Says: (11:52:39 PM)
HEY—did U take a blood sample out of my arm???????????

Cathy Says: (11:52:48 PM)
VICTOR?

Emma says: (11:53:06 PM)
    ?   Is there a reason he
    might think U had cancer?

Cathy Says: (11:52:59 PM)
        Victor?

Cathy says: (11:53:14 PM)
    <no answer from V>

Emma says: (11:53:52 PM)
    Here's what's weird. If U =
    "C", the 2nd sample on Jan
    28, then U came up Zero on
    the TRAP assay...and he wrote
    DAMN IT in the book. Almost
    like he *wanted* U 2 score
    high.
    What if he was onto, like,
    terrorist bio-weapons—like
    INFECTIOUS CANCER???? What
    if he tried to INFECT YOU!!!!!!!!

Cathy says: (11:54:15 PM)
    EMMA! JEEZ!

Emma says: (11:54:38 PM)
    —dumb idea. Forget I ever
    said that.

Cathy says: (11:54:52 PM)
    Oh, SURE I will. np....

Feb 5, Really Awfully Late
(Hour of You-Should-Be Asleep-Only-It's-Very-Important-to-Think-About Anything-That-Isn't-Injectable-Cancer)

Stared at the cancer research stuff for a while, only then I got deeply creeped out. So then I spent Way Too Long going through the stuff I got from my easier B & E at the airplane hangar. Found a French-to-English translator on the web and typed in the stuff on the wedding invitation.

*

Tried a shortcut and called Victor on my beautiful new dolphin phone. He didn't answer. Big surprise.

God, I'm tired.

*

Tried to sleep but couldn't quite make it. I keep thinking about Victor sticking a needle full of cancer in my arm, even though I know he would never do that. Sometimes, just for a change of pace, I imagine the cops showing up on our doorstep to arrest me for breaking into Intrepid, plus I think Mom's Marquis is overdue for its smog inspection. This is California. We take that stuff seriously.

*

Reprogrammed my dolphin phone so instead of playing "Bittersweet Symphony" it has a ring like an old rotary phone from World War II. Emma programmed hers so you just hear her voice saying, "ring?...ring?...ring?..."

What a pair we are.

*

Victor, wherever you are, call me back. I need to know what you did to me. I need to know what you're running from. What about Tsao? Who is he? Should I trust him? *What's going on?*

Call me. Please. Don't leave me alone.

*

Feb 6, Morning
(Recalling Tirehenge)

Woke up early and couldn't get back to sleep. Watched the alarm-clock read-out flash beside my bed: 5:03, 5:04, 5:05…. numbers glowing light-saber blue.

When I was six years old, I discovered that if I climbed up on the porch rail, I could work my way into the cherry tree at the side of our house, and from there I could edge along a branch and scramble onto the roof of our garage. I could see into all the neighbor's yards and I was finally taller than the bratty red-headed boy next door. I felt like the queen of the world. Then one day that red-headed kid saw me up there, and said I wouldn't dare jump down. So I did, just to spite him. I broke my ankle doing it, and when I got home from the hospital, I was never allowed on the garage roof again.

My point here is, I started spying on Victor because I was mad that he dumped me. Then I kept at it because Emma told me not to. If I was a *nice* person, I'd probably never get anything done at all.

*

A couple of weeks after our airplane ride, Victor took me out on our first regular Date. He told me he was going to take me out to kind of a swanky restaurant and I said great and then Emma had to listen to me whine about how I had absolutely nothing I could wear. I spent an entire weekend haunting thrift and resale stores until I found this incredible dress, a third-hand Chloé, black silk, with a cuuuurrrrvy fitted bodice. My pulse actually raced when I picked it off the rack behind a grim regiment of Gap Originals. My boobs weren't quite up to the job of filling out the dress like it ought to be filled, but skinny is always chic, right? I sure wasn't going to miss the chance to buy a thousand dollar dress for the price of the All You Can Eat Buffet at Sizzler.

The restaurant was gorgeous, the Asian-French cuisine incredible, my date obnoxious. Actually, the real trouble didn't start until the dessert (cinnamon-dusted profiteroles for him, mango crème brulee for me). I was smart and funny and completely together from the time they brought the shrimp pot-stickers in mint sauce to the moment they cleared away the poached salmon in coconut milk. Only at dessert, toying with my mango crème brulee, did my nerve break. "So — *Abort, Cathy! Abort!* "So, um, do you like the dress?"

Drat. I wanted to impale my own tongue on my dessert fork.

Victor looked at me, amused. "It's a lovely dress."

Whew.

He speared one of the little chocolate cream puffs on his dessert plate. "It doesn't suit you very well, but that's not the *dress's* fault."

Sometimes, in a world full of phonies, Victor's weird bluntness struck me as strong and admirable. This was not one of those times. "Oh—so you're a fashion critic, now? Got a lot of back issues of *Vogue* lying around the lab?" I said, loudly enough that the couple at the next table turned to look at us.

Victor shrugged. "Hey, I know enough to know you want to emphasize your best features, rather than…" Our fellow diners watched as he waved his spoon at my chest—my flat, flushing chest, as highlighted by the Chloé's open upper bodice. "I mean, you don't want to draw attention to what you haven't got, right?"

One table over, a curvy tramp in an ice-blue Donna Karan flicked a glance at her date and suppressed a smile. Hot waves of embarrassment crawled over me so intensely I thought my knobby collarbones were going to burst into flames.

"For instance, I don't have six-pack abs," Victor went on, oblivious. "So I'm not going to go around wearing one of those muscle shirts that ends over my belly button. The French would say, if I think I've got a fat gut, I ought to direct attention somewhere else."

I tried to think of a witty comeback, but I couldn't come up with one, so I picked up my crème brûlée and dumped it on his head.

Victor made a strangled yawping noise, like a parrot being rolled under a heavily loaded shopping cart. I thought it was a really cute little noise. I was hoping he would make it again, but he just sat in his chair, paralyzed, as burnt custard trickled slowly down his face. A wave of nervous laughter tittered around the tables next to us.

"Nobody's looking at your stomach," I pointed out.

Victor reached up and thoughtfully wiped the crème brulee from around his eyes. "Thanks," he said.

"Oh, geez," I said, frowning. "But now they're staring at your face!"

"Worse and worse," he said drily, signaling our waiter. "I'd like a wet towel and the check, please."

MMMWWWAHAHAHA . . . .

"Certainly, sir." The waiter examined the large lump of custard still quivering on the top of Victor's head, and then turned to me, superbly deadpan. "I hope you found the dessert satisfactory?"

"It was perfect," I said.

*

Victor excused himself to get cleaned up in the restaurant washroom. It seemed to take an awfully long time, and I had visions of trying to walk the twenty-five miles back to Burlingame in my strappy dress sandals. But when he finally came back, his hair pushed back, sleek and wet as an otter's, he was smiling. The people at the tables around us smirked and twittered, but he still really didn't seem to give a damn about them, which made it easier for me not to give a damn either. "Not a lot of things surprise me," he said. "But you surprise me all the time."

"Are you going to give me a ride home? Or should I start hitch-hiking?"

"Promise not to spit or throw or pour things on me?"

"No promises," I said.

He drove me home. I wasn't quite comfortable, yet, with having him in the house, but I didn't want the evening to be over, either, so I made him wait on the curb while I changed into jeans and a big, chunky hooded sweatshirt and then we went for a walk. We stopped at the 7-Eleven and got a couple of IBC root beers, the ones that come in glass bottles. The stoner checkout guy carded Victor, and Victor said he was from out of state and how old did a guy have to be to buy root beer in Cali anyway? :-/

We walked to my ancient tribal hunting grounds, Roosevelt Elementary School, and slipped through the play structure to the sandpit, which was broken up by giant monster truck tires, some toppled on their sides, others towering nine feet out of the sand. Tirehenge, we used to call it. Victor and I scrambled up the tallest tire and sat on top drinking root beer together. Somehow I started talking about my Dad. It was the first time I'd talked about him, really, since the funeral.

I started talking and I couldn't stop, things kept spilling out of me… the Swiss Army knife he gave me for my ninth birthday; the time I dumped nail polish remover on one of his paintings; how I used to dread coming home to him on report card days. My marks were such a jumble—he used to say the teachers

92.

must have picked them up at a garage sale for cheap. I didn't always do so well on Effort and Attitude, either. I told Victor about the mobile of color wheels Dad hung over my crib, and how he taught me to recognize seven different kinds of ducks, and how the day before he died I had blown off dinner with my folks to hang at Emma's place. And all that talking got mixed up with crying, tears and words spilling over one another…

I sat on that tire in the darkness and cried until my root beer tasted salty. I was shaking and shaking, just another bit of wreckage on the flood, trying not to let the river of grief roll me under.

Victor put his arm around me. In the middle of crying I laughed, a little wet hiccup. He asked what was funny. "Your cologne. Burnt custard."

"Next year, *everyone* will be wearing it."

I was so grateful for his arm around my body. I leaned into him, the warmth of his side against mine. He made that lonesome sound you make by blowing over the top of a bottle. "Death comes down like twilight," Victor said. "Everything going gray. Getting darker all the time." He said, "There was this time—"

He stopped.

"What?" He shook his head. "Come on," I said.

He blew softly over the bottle again. "I was standing on this plain. Bodies everywhere. And it felt as if they were draining the color out of the world. Bleeding it into the ground."

"Oh, my God."

"It was a place called Alashgerd." He stirred, leaving a memory. I could practically hear the roll of shutters coming down behind his eyes, the click the doors of his memory made as they swung firmly shut. "That doesn't matter. I just meant to say, the world went dim for a while after that."

Some time later I said, "I just want to feel like I did before."

"It's never going to happen," Victor said softly. The night air smelled just faintly of crème brulee. "Things are never the same after you come to know death. But it won't always seem this dark."

The shaking rush in my chest slowly subsided. The firm pressure of his arm around my shoulder was holding me together. "Will it get better?"

"Cathy, you burn like a candle in the dark." Victor tilted up my face with his

93.

fingers. "All your life, people are going to see that, even from far away, even in the middle of the night, and they are going to come to you." He touched my damp cheek, still wet with tears. I could feel my skin flushing against his fingers. "They are going to want to add your light to theirs," he said. "And every night ends, and then it's morning, and the sun comes up."

"Kiss me," I said.

"I shouldn't," he whispered: but he started to anyway. And if my Mom hadn't called on my cell phone right then, I bet he would have.

She wanted me to pick up some groceries for breakfast. She reminded me of some homework I had due. Probably she was using some Sinister Superpower mothers develop to frustrate any daughters out with boys late at night. Once she hung up, I tried to get back to the kissing part, but Victor was already climbing down the tire and it would have felt lame to try to lure him back up again. At the time I thought he was trying to be a gentleman—trying (irritatingly) not to take advantage of me in a vulnerable moment. Now, knowing what I do about Giselle, and Bianca, and his condition… Maybe I'm just flattering myself, but I don't think it was only me he was trying to protect. In my secret heart, I think I wasn't the only one in danger of falling in love.

*

Cathy, you burn like a candle in the dark.

It's hard to let go of someone who would say that to you, even once.

Feb 6, Still Morning, and Pretty Darn Early at That (Hour of the Palmolive Martini)

I still didn't know what to do about Victor and I was tired of crying, so I went into the kitchen and made myself a gin & tonic. God, that stuff is vile. The first sip was a vivid flashback to last week—puking my guts out at three AM—so I poured the rest of my drink down the sink. Then, on impulse, I grabbed the Gordon's bottle and dumped the rest of the gin too, and chased it with dish detergent until the sink didn't smell like juniper berries any more.

Came back here to make some notes on the Victor mystery but found myself playing Free Cell on the computer instead.

—Car just rolled into the driveway. No flashing lights or sirens, so I guess it's

Mom getting home from her shift. She must be so tired.

Feb 6, Morning

(Hour of the French Toast Breakfast)

Mom came in quietly, trying not to wake me (if only!). I shuffled out to say hi and we sat together at the kitchen table, me in my PJs and her in sweatpants and a woolly sweater. "Why don't you ever wear your uniform home?" I put some water on to boil for peppermint tea. "If I were you, I'd just pitch face-first across my bed in my scrubs."

"The hospital smell." Mom slipped off her shoes and rubbed one aching foot. "Also hygiene. Lots of germs in a hospital. We get a lot of sick people there, you know."

Hospital smell, I thought. "That's why you never really liked it when Dad got you flowers," I said slowly. "Because you see flowers at the hospital all the time."

She looked up at me unhappily. "It didn't show, did it?"

"I don't think he noticed."

"I loved the thought, Cathy."

Mom's toes wriggled at the bottom of her industrial strength pantyhose. "It's just … God, I throw out a lot of rotten flowers, you know? You get to the point, you start betting yourself who's going to make it longer, the patient or the roses. You don't think your father noticed, do you?"

I said, "I'm sure he didn't."

She sighed. "He always thought you two were closer. He didn't want to hurt my feelings by saying it out loud, but that's what he thought. The truth is, you're a lot more like me than you are like him."

She put her aching feet back on the floor and walked over to the tall cabinet with the tea and coffee on the middle shelf and the booze on the top. She looked up to where the gin bottle ought to be but wasn't.

"I'm making some tea," I said. "Want some?"

She pried her eyes away from the bottles on the top shelf and snuck a glance at me. Ashamed. "Sure." She closed the cabinet door. "We should have breakfast. It seems like we never have breakfast together anymore. Why is that?"

We both knew.

"I should make something," she said. "I should make us something for breakfast." She stood at the counter, at a loss.

The kettle boiled and I poured hot water into the teapot. "I could make some French toast."

"I can do it, sweetie."

I sat her back down at the kitchen table. "You take care of people all night. Let someone take care of you for once."

"French toast sounds great." My mother looked at me. Her eyes were wet. "Why are you being so nice to me?"

*

I put a skillet on the stove for French toast and cracked eggs into a plate. "Was it worth it?" I said, smushing them up with a fork, keeping my back turned so we wouldn't have to look at one another. "Being married to dad. Are you glad you did it—now, after everything?"

"If I hadn't married him, there'd be no *you*," she said. "I'd hate to think of a planet with no Cathy on it to jump off the garage roof."

"Boy, are you ever going to let me forget about that?"

"If it wasn't for your dad…I don't know what my life would have meant." She looked into the depths of her peppermint tea. "I don't know what it means now, now that he's gone. I look at the future and it seems…I don't know. Empty and confusing."

I dunked a slice of bread into the egg batter and then dropped it into the skillet, where it lay on its tummy and hissed at me.

Mom rubbed the tears out her eyes the same way I do. The same angry swipe with the back of her hand. "What I do know, is that without my support for Dad's work, the United States Postal Service would never have had a truly excellent Bufflehead Duck Stamp."

"It's a good stamp," I said.

"A *damn* good stamp," Mom said.

I turned around. We were both crying. Mom wiped her eyes again. "Where's my damn toast?" she said.

Feb 6, Evening
(Lifestyles of the Suddenly Broke)

Emma showed up on my porch just after eight o'clock. There was no warning: just an angry thump on the door and her standing outside, bristling like a wet cat. She was wearing black jeans and a black silk shirt I bought her that she never wore, plus an old jean jacket of mine I thought I'd lost. Her eyes were hard as ball bearings and she had done something to her hair—filled it with little glistening splintery things that made her look vaguely weird and dangerous. She jerked her head at the BMW her Dad had given her for her 16th birthday, which was idling at the curb. "Get in the car."

"Okay," I said. That's what pals do.

"Hey—the Beemer ought to be good for a year's tuition at M.I.T." I said, climbing into the shotgun seat. "It's probably hell to park in Boston anyway."

"It's not my car," she grated.

"What?"

"Turns out Dad leased it. It goes back to the dealership tomorrow. Thought I'd take it out for one last spin," Emma said.

We drove.

The silence started to get to me. "I've decided to do the grown-up thing and stop chasing Victor," I said. We shot out of the last valley on 280. The lights of San Francisco blazed up in front of us. "You were right. You can't make someone love you, and I never really knew him well enough to, you know, break the law." Or risk the kind of heartbreak Mom was going through now.

Emma looked over, surprised. "Is this the girl who got even with Kyle Stuart by putting Krazy Glue inside his bike helmet?"

"I was young! Besides... I've already lost one man in my life this year. That's enough grief for high school." And really, Emma was right. I had a lot of catching up to do at school, a lot of work in the real world. Mom had enough to deal with without me making a car crash out of my life. For that matter, dropping out and condemning myself to a life behind the counter at Starbucks would not have thrilled Dad either. "Recess is over," I said. "Time to go back to school."

"Oh, no you don't," Emma said grimly.

"Don't what?"

"Give up on Victor." She glared at me, and her British accent got thicker as it always did in moments of great emotion. "If you think, after all the time I've spent tracking down this Roaming Romeo of yours, that I intend to let go of the only Individual of High Net Worth we know, you can think again."

I looked at the speedometer. The Beemer was climbing up into the 80s. "You really aren't giving up on this 30/30 thing, are you?"

"We are going to find Victor," Emma grated out, "and then either you are going to marry his butt, or we are going to turn him in and collect a reward."

"You think the cops have a bounty on him?"

"I didn't say it had to be the cops."

"You're joking, right? Emma?"

She gave me a look. "Of course I'm joking, you stupid cow. You don't have to marry him," she said. "You could live in sin. Doesn't matter to me, as long as you get checkbook privileges."

"Oh. That's great, then." My stomach growled. "I guess you've probably eaten already."

"Dad said we should go out to dinner and I said we didn't have any money. He said we could put it on my credit card. I panicked." Emma glowered at the dark freeway unwinding in front of her (leased) halogen headlamps. "He sits there all day watching stock prices and calling his cronies. Their secretaries won't put him through and they never call him back, but he says everything's going to be fine, just fine." She glanced at me. "I said I would make him a nice home-made meal."

"Oh, dear." I had experienced enough of Emma's cooking to wince. *jump for jo*

"You can't really skin prawns with a potato peeler," she said. "You ought to be able to, but after a while there are all these flimsy bits of carapace clinging to your fingers like torn contact lenses. And legs," Emma said with a shudder. "Little wet grasshopper legs everywhere."

I looked again at the spiky, shiny things in her hair.

OMG.

A real friendship is like a marriage: for richer and poorer, for better and for worse. If the moment of truth comes, and you can't bear to make a sacrifice, what kind of friend are you?

I looked at the bits of prawn tangled in her hair, and gulped. "Hang on a sec," I said. "I've got a comb."

*

I brushed out Emma's hair as we sat in the drive-thru at Burger King, then dropped the comb in the trash on the way out. We ate our burgers while Emma drove into the city, getting off the freeway somewhere near Golden Gate Park. "I have to get a scholarship now," she said, licking Special Sauce off her fingers. "I think my odds would be better if I was on a team."

"You're on Math Olympiad, right?"

"No, I mean a sports team."

I gagged on a french fry.

Emma flushed. "I was thinking about crew," she said, with brittle dignity. "Rowing. There's still time to sign up. They row in Boston, you know. I looked it up. Harvard versus Yale, like the Oxford/Cambridge boat race. I was thinking, those New England schools, M.I.T., I did a 790 on my Math SAT, and if I could row crew, maybe that would give me an edge over the other math nerds."

By this time we were somewhere in the Haight, rolling slowly up a crowded street. The sidewalks were thick with the young and trendy, geared up in leather jackets and eye-brow rings. I chased my French fry with a slug of Coke. "Emma, have you ever rowed a boat?"

"Um…"

"*Sat* in a boat?"

"I saw **TITANIC** eleven times," she said meekly.

"Everybody *drowns!*"

"I can't make the track team," Emma cried. "I'm too short and British."

"Too *British?*" We passed the big Ameoba records store. "Hey," I said suspiciously. Emma turned the Beamer up Victor's street. "*Hey!* Where do you think you're going?"

"We can't give up on Victor now," Emma said. "Not after all the time I put in, researching TRAP assays and Intrepid's corporate history. I could have been working out on a rowing machine," she said resentfully. She smacked her shoulder. "I could have quads out to here."

"Your quads are on your legs."

99.

"Spare me the anatomy lesson. The point is, I could have been preparing for the spring races. Did you know they call them heads? Head of the Port. That's what they call the big meet in Sacramento. Hello, my name is Emma Cheung, I do great Heads."

"EMMA! Get a grip. This is so unfair! You were the one who told me to stay out of Victor's business. You were the one who said I would get hurt. You were the one who said I should start acting my age and pay attention to my schoolwork."

"Oh, right," she said, rolling her eyes. "Like you're going to get a scholarship to Stanford."

"Hey—"

"YES! YES, I SAID ALL THOSE THINGS! But that was before *Dad*," she hissed. We reached the top of the block. Emma jerked the BMW up against the curb. "You were right all along. You can't predict anything in this life. One minute, you're rounding up venture capital—the next, you've got shrimp legs up your nose. You can lose everything in a heartbeat."

"You haven't lost *everything*—"

"—And in a world like that, if you can't count on your friends," she said, "what can you count on?" She looked at me, eyes bright with tears. "Your friend might be in a lot of trouble," she said. "This friend—Victor, you know—this friend might really need you."

It slowly dawned on me that this was Emma's way of saying, *Thanks,* and *Sorry,* and *I'm glad you're here.*

We sat together in the dark. Finally the leather upholstery squeaked as Emma shifted, starting to get out. "Emma! This is crazy!"

"So call the cops." She forced herself out of the car and walked up to the gate at the bottom of Victor's property. Despite all her tough talk, she dithered on the sidewalk. Geez—the poor kid was practically raised by nuns, after all.

This would be the cue for Hardened Break-&-Enter Grrl to make her entrance. I sighed and got out of the car. "Don't just stand there," I murmured. "You look like a freaking criminal. Yeah," I said loudly, for the benefit of anyone listening, "this is the address all right." And grabbing Emma's arm, I whisked her through the gate.

"You're really good at this," Emma squeaked.

100.

"Practice makes perfect." We followed the white gravel path up to the house. There was a light on in one of the front rooms, but otherwise the house was dark. "That light is just there to scare burglars," I said.

"It's working on me," Emma said.

"Who's the tough guy now?"

"Finding Victor is my best rational plan. That's what I'm doing," Emma hissed. "So sue me if I don't have your natural criminal instincts."

The front door was locked. The back door was locked too, but it didn't matter so much after I borrowed my jean jacket back from Emma and wrapped it around my fist and punched the glass out. "Jesus!" Emma squeaked. "Did you have to be so *loud?*"

"It's *glass*," I said, equally freaked out. Somehow when they do that it in the movies there's one muffled crash and then the bad guys slither into the home undetected, but when I did it, it sounded as if I had hurled a bowling ball through a line of patio doors.

very suave

It took a great effort of will to unscrew my closed eyes and ungrit my clenched teeth. "Oops!" I said, loudly again, just in case someone was still listening. "We should get a broom and clean that up," I said.

Emma was staring at me and muttering under her breath. "Why do I let you get me mixed up in these things...."

"*Me?* It was you who—"

But she had already reached through the broken door, turned the knob, and let herself into Victor's kitchen. It was pitch black. Broken glass crunched under our feet. "Let's try the study," I said quietly. "Maybe we can find another phone number, or numbers."

"Oof!" There was a whump and a bang in front of me, and then Emma was swearing quietly and continuously in Cantonese.

"What happened?"

"Stupid butcher block island kitchen design THING," she sputtered.

"This is ridiculous." I fumbled around until I found a light switch. Classy contemporary lighting flooded the kitchen with a soft, even light, perfect for meal preparation.

"Isn't this a little conspicuous, Cathy?"

"I think we're pretty much past stealth," I said dryly. "If someone comes, we'll go with the demented girlfriend excuse."

"It's got the ring of truth, anyway."

I told her not to leave fingerprints on anything and led her to the study at the front of the house. Victor's desk was not the mess it had been last time. The top was tidy and his computer was gone. "Empty, empty, empty," I said, trying the desk drawers. "Rubber bands and supplies, blank writing paper … Ah," I said, testing the bottom drawer on the right. "Papers!" I pulled up a handful. "Nothing new, though," I said, disappointed. "Mostly old letters, it looks like. More souvenirs. And this looks like … a restaurant menu? Why on earth would he have a paper placemat from the Bad Penny Saloon?" I said, holding the thing up, perplexed.

"Hm?"

Emma clearly hadn't been following what I was saying. She was staring, rapt, at the Chagall painting.

I couldn't help grinning. Great art is like that. You can think you're a real hard-ass, with no use for artsy-fartsy jazz—and then one of the greats hits you like a bullet through the heart. People talk about Tiger Woods, or Michael Jordan—but if you *really* want to see a dude playing above the rim, spend half an hour looking at Picassos from between the wars. The greats don't just want to score—they want to dunk in your face. It was nice to see Chagall slam down on Miss Junior Business Achievement Club. "Gorgeous, isn't it?"

"How…" Emma breathed. She dragged her gaze from the painting and looked at me with wonder in her eyes. "*How much* did you say that thing was worth?"

"Hey. Whoa. We're here to find Victor, remember?"

"The heck with Victor!" Emma cried. "Six hundred thousand dollars—are you joking? Four years at M.I.T. with my own apartment and enough left over to send my Dad back to HK for the duration!" She grinned. "And we don't have to get mixed up with the drug dealer!" She reached up for the painting.

I grabbed her arms. "*Whoa.* Break-&-Enter Grrl didn't sign up for Grand Theft. Stalking Victor is romantic, remember? That's what a jury would think. Stealing that painting is 7-to-10 in a women's prison with a cell-mate named Butch."

"I'm not talking Grand Theft," Emma said mutinously. "I just think we should pinch it, that's all."

"You really want to stagger around Haight-Ashbury with a framed Chagall?"

"You're right. You're right," Emma said. "I don't know what I was thinking. The frame would look suspicious. I'll get a knife from the kitchen and cut it out," she said brightly.

"You … will … not … hurt … that … painting," I grated. Emma made a Huffy Face as I guided her hands away from the painting and set them back on Victor's desk, next to a little black box, barely the size of a pack of matches. "That's weird. This wasn't here last time." I picked the box up, but it didn't seem to have a lid, or button, or anything. "What do you suppose it does?"

Emma's eyes widened, and she looked across the study. Sitting on a bookshelf across from the desk was an identical little plastic box. "Uh-oh."

I put the box down.

"Hard to say for sure," Emma said carefully, "but I would guess that was an infra-red motion detector."

"As in a burglar alarm?" My mouth was dry.

"That's what I was thinking."

"Maybe Victor left it," I said. I started shoveling papers from Victor's bottom drawer into my purse.

"Maybe," Emma said. "Or maybe someone else did. Either way, it would have gone off as soon as we stepped inside this room. If there were dispatchers monitoring it, they would have called the cops already."

"Right. So plan B, remember, is the jealous girlfriend."

"Right," Emma said. "What was plan A again?"

"Run like hell."

We were halfway down the gravel path when we heard a car come up the hill and stop at the bottom of Victor's grounds. I dragged Emma off the path and back behind a stand of bamboo. We squatted in the darkness as two car doors clunked shut below. I held a finger over Emma's lips, and together we wiggled very, very quietly deeper into the shadows as footsteps started up the gravel path toward the house.

I put my hand on Emma's shoulder, holding her still as the footsteps got closer. Two sets. A man's voice came in the darkness. "Flashlights?"

"No," said his buddy. "Let's try not to spook whoever's up there." His voice was older. Deeper.

"You don't think it's him?"

"He's not stupid enough to trigger the alarm," the old cop said.

I stayed completely frozen. The men were passing us now. Dark pants, dark shirts—cops. I could see the glint of badges at chest level, and the bump on the hip of the nearest guy where his gun was holstered.

OMG.

"You think it's the girlfriend?"

"No sign of the piece-of-crap Mercury," the old cop said.

"She could have taken the bus." The voices began to dwindle, continuing up the hill. "The old man said she does that sometimes."

How the hell did they know this stuff about me?

I turned my head and found Emma staring at me, wide-eyed. I felt her shoulder quivering under my hand. "Wait until they're in the house," I mouthed.

She nodded, trusting to my superior criminal skills.

A short time later we heard footsteps on the porch, and then another light came on in the house. We snuck out from behind the screen of bamboo. We tried to creep down the path for about ten seconds, tiptoeing and shushing one another. Then our nerves broke and we sprinted wildly down the path, jumped into the Beemer like Bonny and Clyde running from a bank job, and shot off for home.

Feb 7, Morning
(Hour of the Fateful Plunge)

I dropped Emma off at her place, with $30 bucks worth of take-out Chinese to keep her dad going. By the time I got home I was still so strung out on adrenaline I had to play minesweeper on the computer for an hour before I could even look at the stuff I'd scooped out of Victor's drawers. It was mostly letters and old newspaper clippings—family history. For some reason, he was obsessed with family history.

I thought of what Tsao had said, about Victor's illness, and his habit of running out on people. Maybe the older man was lying, but maybe not. Maybe you think a lot about the past, when you haven't got much future in front of you.

Just past eleven o'clock I called Tsao, and told him Victor would meet him the next day (today as I write) at the Musée Mécanique at 11.

Now it's morning and I'm trying to decide if I'm going to spy on them.

*

Jesus, Cathy—weren't you just saying it's time to grow up? Just one time, do the smart thing: catch the bus to school, sit quietly in class, and forget all about Victor's secret project and Carla Beckman's gunshot wounds and *Cemetery Gates*. It will take an effort, but you can do it, I know you can.

Yeah, sure, right.

Feb 7—no, 8, actually, it's past midnight
(Hour of "Holy Sh—, ArtGrrl!")

OMG.

It's beejn hours sincee I got home but forr the longrest time m hands were shakking to badly to type.

OMG.

Short list fr today:

- kidnaspping, death threats, Victor, copds, truth abouyt the neeedle in my arm, knives—

*

stuipisd shhakingf hhands.

*

OK, what dumb broad poured out the gin?

*

Just listened to "Bittersweet Symphony" 9 times in a row. Everything is Under Control.

I meant to write down what happened but that's hard when I'm this wired, so I took out a pad and did sketches first—the mountain hideout, the cops, the sword, the terminal kid (that's how I thought of her before I realized *I was terminal, too*). Calmed my hands down, which is good. Pencil for me = cop's gun. We all feel better with a weapon in hand....

So I'm just going to write it down. Obivously I'm making up some of the exact words people said but it's all pretty close. Want to do it now, while everythings fresh. Write it down, send it to someone smart, send it to Emma tomorrow, ask her what to do.

For right now, don't think. Just write and draw. write and draw.

*

This morning—so of course I had to spy on Victor and Tsao—

...I splurged and took the car down to Pier 45, which was a big mistake. I finally had to park on Chestnut for $5/hr, and promise to be back at 1:00. Not by one—at one. The valets double park all the cars, and God help you if you're early.

I trotted down Powell to Jefferson and hurried along Fisherman's Wharf, wrapped in my jean jacket and my Secret Agent Sunglasses, for Extra Disguise Value. I hurried past Bush Man, the weird guy at Pier 43 who hides behind the lamp-poles and jumps out at people. For some reason tourists from places like Nebraska and Indiana find this cute enough to throw a steady trickle of change into his hat. Makes you wonder exactly what they do for fun in Lincoln on a Saturday night. The Wharf was fairly empty as I bustled along, and I saw Bush Man begin a little furtive stalking, but I glared at him over my sunglasses and reached into my purse as if going for a bottle of pepper spray. He jumped back like he recognized the gesture. I guess we get tourists from New York, too.

I slowed up as I got to the Ripley's *Believe it Or Not!* Museum, where my dad took me once to see the two-headed calf, the eight foot stegosaurus made entirely from chrome bumpers, and what they advertised as a "self-portrait of Van Gogh made from toasted bread!" We both went on a toast-carving binge for weeks afterward. Crumbs everywhere.

10:27, according to my watch. I had wanted to be in position by 10:15. Rats.

I hurried onto the Pier proper, hoping I could find a hiding place from which to stake out the entrance to the Musée Mécanique. For once, something came easy. Docked right next to the pier is the *Pampanito*, a WWII sub now open to the public. I paid my entrance fee and scampered on board. There were only a couple of people wandering around, and I had a brief fantasy of staking out Pier 45 through the periscope—how would that be for surveillance? But sooner or later someone would come and kick me off, so I went low-tech, creeping up to crouch on the seaward side of the conning tower, keeping watch from behind the radar masts.

Victor showed up two minutes later. He had to be related to Tsao—same features, same walk. Same solitary quality, too; as if he were the only living person in a city of ghosts.

Victor slowed as he came to the Musée. For one heart-stopping moment I thought he was going to come on board the *Pompanito* for the same reason I had, and the whole gig would collapse into slapstick, with me scurrying around the sub from periscope to radar tower. Thankfully, Victor decided to step into the area next to the Musée, the doorway of the City of San Francisco Museum.

A moment later, a couple of uniformed cops came strolling up the pier. I froze. No way these were going to just happen to be the same guys who almost caught me and Emma last night, right? And yet … the fact that those guys had known so much about me was deeply creepy.

A white winged gull settled on the *Pompanito*'s forward gun. It cocked its head and eyed me steadily. Victor slid into the City Museum. The cops ambled on toward the end of the pier.

Tsao appeared, walking fast, posture immaculate. He pushed through the door to the Musée Mécanique. Victor stepped out of the City Museum and followed him inside.

I swore. The gull opened his yellow beak in a long, insolent yawn. "Screw you," I said. "I'm not going in there. They'll see me if I go in there."

108.

The gull fluffed his feathers.

"Plus there's the cops," I said. "Jeez. Come on. Be reasonable."

The gull hopped a couple of times on the *Pompanito*'s forward gun, shook out his wings, and screeched at me.

"Okay! Fine! Whatever!" I stood up and edged around the radar towers, figuring with my luck Victor would come popping out the front door at any instant, but he didn't. I hurried to the gangway. The gull jeered at me as I hurried away from him. "You're a rotten winner," I said.

No sign of the cops. I crossed the pier as fast as I could and hurried into the Musée. It was dim inside. I couldn't see Victor or Tsao.

Laughing Sal, the gap-toothed clown girl, cackled at me and waved her mechanical arm cheerily at the rest of the exhibits. There was the Masked Strongman I had arm-wrestled when Victor brought me here, Grand-Ma the Fortune-Teller, a couple of "orchestrions"—player pianos with whistles and gongs and flutes added in—an automated Barber Shop Quartet, an ancient pinball machine, a model baseball game from 1927, and, across the entrance from Sal, a carved dwarf sitting on a chair with the grumpy expression of a man who knows that everyone is laughing at him.

I kept my head down, pretending to rummage for something in my purse while waiting for my eyes to adjust to the dim light. The only other people in the front room with me were two girls, one blond and about twelve, the other dark-haired and maybe eight. From the way they were bickering, I assumed they were sisters. The younger one wanted to spend some more quarters slugging it out with the K.O. Boxers; the older girl wanted to hear the Barber Shop Quartet.

I could just see the back of Tsao's expensive suit jacket one room further in.

I really didn't want to get caught. Now that I was here, I was remembering all over again that Carla Beckman had *died* for sticking her nose where it didn't belong. My body had that stage-fright feeling—clammy hands, sick tension in the stomach, heart beating too fast. I slunk deeper into the Musée, careful to keep on the edges of the room. I worked my way next to the dwarf (who turned out to be a Lucky Irish Leprechaun, although you wouldn't guess it to look at his expression). I pretended to read the long signboard of blarney underneath his chair, but actually I was throwing my whole attention into my ears. I could just hear Tsao and

[handwritten margin note:] note self ↓ try n to forg th

Victor talking. Tsao's voice was calm and authoratitive, Victor's sharp and angry.

Victor: "<mutter mutter> didn't *know?*"

Tsao: <calming>

Victor: "<mutter> find *out!*"

Tsao: <question?>

Victor: "<mutter> on Lucky, on Bianca—all of them. You don't just…*forget.*"

Tsao: <question>

*

Someone tapped me on the back and I nearly jumped through the ceiling. It was the two sisters. I stood there, white and gasping, probably looking like the Evil Queen when she finds out Snow White is still alive. "We need quarters," the little sister said, holding up a dollar bill.

The older sister looked embarrassed. "Rosie, I'm sure there's a change machine—"

"She might have some quarters—"

"It's not *polite*—"

I grabbed some quarters from my purse and shoved them into the dark-haired girl's hand. "There you go." I glanced down the corridor. Tsao and Victor were walking even deeper into the building.

The little brown-haired girl tapped me on the back again. "*What?*" I hissed.

"Why are you wearing sunglasses inside?" The reason my ideas are not always the brightest?

I flushed and took off my shades. The Musée suddenly didn't seem quite so dark. The girls exchanged eyerolls and trooped back toward the KO Boxers.

I eased into the second room of the Musée and pretended to be intensely interested in a mechanical chrome horse as I resumed my eavesdropping. Tsao was doing more of the talking. His tone was calm, perhaps even slightly reproving, but he kept his voice low. He was facing away from me, and it was nearly impossible to make out more than a word or two. "Eight" "ribs" …"brawl", or maybe that was "roll"…?

Victor made a sarcastic comment about sending a card.

I figured they must be talking about the fight outside the Eight Ancestors restaurant. But how had Tsao known about that?

Tsao said something in a warning tone of voice. It sounded like, *police*.

"I stay away from the cops," Victor said.

Tsao stepped toward me, idly inspecting one of the displays. I quickly turned my back and leaned in to study the chrome horse as if I wanted to jump on its back.

"Not regular police," Tsao said. "*Special* police."

#

Someone tapped me on the back again. If I were a cartoon character, I would have had to peel myself off the ceiling. This time it was the blond twelve year old sister. "Excuse me," she said.

"I haven't got any more quarters!" I hissed. "What are you guys even *doing* here? Shouldn't you be in school?"

The blonde girl's eyebrows rose. "We didn't ask *you* that."

"If you want to listen, hide in the Mandarin," said the dark-haired one named Rosie. I blinked. She glanced over at an exhibit at the end of the room. It was a fake Pagoda, surrounded by black velvet curtains, in front of which a signboard read:

ask THE MANDARIN!

Love!

Wealth!

Happiness!

SEEK OUT THE ANCIENT WISDOM OF THE ORIENT!

"Nobody knows you're behind the curtains," the little girl explained. "Then you wouldn't be so jumpy."

Her big sister nodded. "Rosie's good at hiding. We used to call her the Stealth Baby."

"We were going to play the barber shop quartet," Rosie added. "Only we figured you wouldn't be able to hear."

"Uh … thanks."

The blond girl grinned. "No problem. Hey Rose, I'll play you a game of baseball!"

The two of them darted back to the front of the museum. Feeling like an idiot, I sidled around the edge of the room and slipped behind the black velvet curtain of The Mandarin.

There was a mannequin, of course, but instead of the sumptuously dressed Confucian sage I had expected, the Mandarin was actually a rumpled-looking, pot-bellied old vagabond with a merry twinkle in his eye and bits of bracken in his white beard. In one hand, he held a bamboo tube drum; in the other, a peach. He was riding backwards on a white donkey. I would swear on my father's grave that his eyes were closed when I stepped through the curtain, but as I dropped into the supplicant's chair before him, they opened in a long, considering stare.

Time slowed.

One mechanical eyelid winked at me.

Time stopped.

#

Images misted slowly in my brain, like steam fogging a window: the paper-folding man. The pawn shop. Hell money rustling. Hoof-beats in the kitchen.

And here, now, everywhere, faintly, the fragrance of peaches.

#

Time started up at the sound of Tsao's voice not five feet away. "They all have to die, Victor."

He must be standing just on the other side of the black velvet curtain. I froze.

"Your wife. Your daughter. That nice girl you've been seeing, Cathy," Tsao said regretfully. "They all have to die, and you know it."

"And you won't do anything to stop it?" Victor said angrily.

"There's nothing to be done." Tsao moved off, heading for the front of the store. "Of course it hurts. You'll get over it. One always does. I don't advise being there at the end. The first few times, you feel as if it comforts them, but in the long run you're better off making a clean break and letting nature take its course."

"You're very good at that, aren't you?"

"At least we have each other," Tsao said dryly. "That counts for something. Oh, it is *wearing*, Victor—you think I don't know that? Day after day of looking into their eyes, listening to them talk, too stupid, all of them, to realize they're as good as dead already. Oneself too polite to remind them, of course... I sometimes think if it weren't for family, I should go mad."

"I'll never be like you," Victor said.

They all have to die

Tsao laughed. "Too late."

Their footsteps dwindled. A moment later I heard the door of the Musée swing open, letting in a quick breath of fresh air and the cry of gulls.

#

I sat in front of the Mandarin, shaking violently. *Your wife. Your daughter. That nice girl you've been seeing, Cathy. They all have to die.*

"Oh, my God," I whispered.   *... and you know it. ...*

The old Chinese mannequin winked again. Gears clanked and whirred. His hand reached out, holding a little roll of parchment wrapped in a cheap red ribbon. The fingers opened and the scroll clanked down into a chute in front of me, like a candy bar falling from a vending machine. I reached down to pick it up. I started to undo the ribbon, but my hands were shaking so hard I couldn't undo the knot for a second.

The black curtain jerked back and I spun around. "For heaven's sake, girls—next time bring a roll of quarters when you…" The words died in my throat. It wasn't the sisters. It was the two cops I had watched amble down the pier.

"Miss Vickers?" the older one said. "You're wanted on charges of criminal trespass and possible industrial espionage at the Intrepid Biotech Corporate offices."

#

They were the same two cops who had come to Victor's house last night. This time it wasn't dark and I wasn't hiding in a bamboo thicket, so I could attach faces to their voices. The older one was in his forties, with a doughy beer-and-pizza body and eyes the color of Budweiser. The younger cop was strictly a side-salad and Perrier guy: Asian, in terrific shape, and good-looking, too, in a SuperCuts Hair Model kind of way.

Perrier read me my rights, just like they do on TV.

"Surprised to see us?" Budweiser wrapped his big fingers around my arm and hauled me to my feet. I yelped. "My turn to be bad cop, sweetie."

"You were the bad cop last time," Perry complained.

Bud started ambling for the lobby of the Musée, jerking me along after him. "Is that right?" he said thoughtfully. "My turn seems to come up a lot."

*

Two blocks from the pier Perry pushed me firmly into the back seat of an unmarked Ford Crown Victoria. "I wasn't—ow! ~~spying! I got into Intrepid~~ *spy fiction* because I wanted to see my crummy ex-boyfriend. Believe me, I wouldn't know a secret formula if it bit me on the butt."

"Not based on the marks you've been getting in Biology," Bud agreed. *non-fiction*

"You should study harder," Perry added disapprovingly, sliding into the passenger side seat up front. "You want to get a good job, you need to pay attention to your education." *horror-fiction !!*

"You've been reading my report cards?" The blood drained out of my face, leaving me cold and clammy. "So you know where I live. How did you find me today? Did you put a bug on my car? Or my clothes?"

Perry turned and stared at me. "Do up your seat belt."

Bud started to drive. My mind was racing like a rabbit through a minefield; every new thought another explosion of shame or fear. I could just imagine my mother getting the call from the cops. She'd have to phone the hospital and cancel her shift. Then her car would be gone—abandoned in Valet parking at $5/hour!—and she'd have to take a cab into San Francisco. God, she was going to be mad.

And disappointed.

For the first time in months we'd actually connected, over French toast this morning. And now this. I could just see the pinch in her face, the bitter set of her mouth when she came to the police station. One more expensive disaster thanks to her irresponsible daughter.

Bud drove up Van Ness, then jumped on to 101 and took it over to 80.

Hunh?

"Where are we going? I mean, haven't we passed the San Francisco police stations?"

"The crime was not committed in San Francisco," Perry said.

"But aren't you San Francisco cops? You'd have to be, wouldn't you, to be walking around San Francisco in uniform? So I expected to go to a San Francisco police station." Bud exited onto 280. "You're taking me home to talk to my Mom, aren't you?" Relief flooded my body, and I sagged back into the Crown Victoria's upholstery. I wasn't looking forward to the conversation with Mom, but it beat being arrested— *barely.*

Wait a sec.

—Why would San Francisco cops bug a car in Burlingame because of a break-and-enter in San Jose? "You must actually be San Jose cops, right? But if you knew where I lived, why didn't you just knock on the door as soon as you found our house…." I trailed off. 280 poured under us, a long grey river. "You're not taking me home, are you?"

No answer.

"I'd like to see your badges, please."

Perry turned around and looked at me from the front seat. "If I showed you a piece of tin I bought this morning at Toys R Us, you wouldn't know the difference."

"I'd like to see them anyway."

No answer.

We passed the Burlingame exits. Bud stayed on 280. The scared feeling in my stomach got worse.

"This is about Victor, isn't it? And we aren't going to Burlingame, we're going to San Jose. We're going back to Intrepid."

Why wouldn't they show me their badges?

"You are real cops," I breathed. "You have real badges with real names on them, or ID numbers, or something, and you don't want me to see them. Because you're doing something wrong," I said. "This isn't police work at all. Intrepid paid you to pick me up."

Perry turned around again. "Gee, Miss Vickers. If you're right, that would mean we couldn't let you tell anybody about this ride. *Ever.*" His eyes were black as the mouth of a revolver.

Bud sighed. "Your turn to be the bad cop after all."

*

We passed the exit to Intrepid. "Hey," I said. No answer. A few minutes later we left the San Jose city limits, heading south. "You can't do this. This is kidnapping."

"We like to think of it more like parcel delivery," Bud said.

A green mileage sign flashed by on the shoulder, listing the distances to Gilroy, Hollister, Monterey.

Monterey. Where they found Carla Beckman's body rolled up on the beach.

"Do either of you have sisters?" I asked. "Or kids? I never had a sister, I'm an only child. My Dad died last year." My voice was shaking and my sweaty palms were slick against the Crown Victoria's vinyl upholstery. I touched Bud's shoulder. "He would have been about your age."

"I wonder what's for dinner tonight," Bud said thoughtfully. "You know what I could go for? Chicken parmesan."

"I'll give you money," I said. "I'll give you anything you want. Just let me out of the car." No answer. "I'm seventeen years old. I don't know anything. I don't know where Victor is. I don't know what he was working on. He's just a guy I met. You don't want to do this. Please. You guys must have sisters, right? Or daughters? Can you imagine waiting, day after day? Wondering if you were ever going to hear from your kid again? Please, don't be part of that. *Please!* Imagine what it would be like."

Bud shifted in his seat. "I need to turn on the damn radio."

Perry turned to face me. "We know exactly what that would be like," he said. "Do you understand? We know *just* how the phone wouldn't ring. We know what the body would look like, later. And we really can't let that happen to … to ours. You see? I'm sorry, Miss Vickers. Really I am. But if your father had to choose between you and some other girl—he would choose you, right?"

"My father would never take someone to die—"

"Your father wasn't asked to make the choice," Perry said patiently. "But if he had to choose, if he really had to, he would save you. Because he loved you. I'm sure he did. And the hard thing is…"

"He should have stuck around," Bud said. "Should have taken better care of himself. He should never have left you. It's a hard world out there. What's a girl to do without someone looking after her?"

"Please," I whispered.

"The thing is," Perry said sadly, "we don't love you."

*

Around San Jose, the hills were bare except for wet grass, green as a frog's back, but thirty minutes later the landscape turned darker as the road turned west, winding through the dim folds of the Coastal Range. Here the hills were wooded with Monterey pines and Van Gogh cypresses. The undergrowth all ferns and poison oak. Just before Prunedale we turned off the highway onto a narrow road, and twisted our way deeper into the secret hills.

The road coiled and twisted, flashing from blank hillsides to dim groves of cypress. I was getting carsick. It would serve the Keystone Kops right if I barfed all over the Ford's plush red upholstery.

...Actually, that was a good idea. That would leave my DNA traces all over. Bud and Perry would have to get the car cleaned. Maybe some car wash guy would remember them coming in.

"I feel sick," I said.

"Sure you do," Bud said. "Listen, honey, this is gonna happen, and nothing you can do—"

I stuck my fingers down my throat. "Uh oh," I croaked. Perry turned to look at me. I barfed copiously, making sure to get plenty up in the front seat.

Bud shouted out a bunch of words you aren't allowed to say on network TV.

I retched again. This time I bent down to get a good splatter under the seats where they'd have a hard time shampooing. *Try to wipe out this evidence, guys.* I came up gasping and spitting.

Bud pulled over. "You. Get out and clean up this car."

"No," Perry said. "If she tries to run, we'll have to shoot her."

"I promise I won't try to run," I said, lying. "Boy. This car sure stinks."

Bud cussed some more and started driving again. He rolled down all four windows. "You're giving me a pain, Cathy."

"Good," I said. *And whatever was going to happen to me I liked the thought of them having to drive home to San Jose in a car that smelled like barf.*

For twenty minutes, the Ford toiled up a long series of switchbacks, rising steadily higher up a tall wooded slope. Normally, twenty minutes of riding in a car stinking of fresh barf would seem like forever. But when you think you might get shot at the end of the ride, the time seems to fly right by.

My hands were sweaty and my heart was racing. My thoughts were rolling around like mercury from a smashed thermometer. At first Mom would think I had run away. She'd be furious and hurt. Then the days would go by without a phone call. The fury would drain away and panic would set in. She'd blame herself for how I turned out. That was one thing about Mom, she only saw herself in the bad things I did. I can still remember those times when some other grown-up would tell her something nice about me, how she would say, "Nothing to do with us! That's just been Cathy since the day she was born." And she would look at me like I was a gift. Like she had been so undeserving, so lucky to have me.

I thought of Emma sneaking down to the weight room in her apartment, looking unhappily at herself in the mirrored walls and trying to figure out how to use the rowing machine. I imagined her joining a rowing team and getting shoulder muscles and learning to wear cool wraparound sunglasses. Maybe she'd meet one of those jocks who falls for smart girls and it was so unfair that I would never get to see it. I would never get to see her race.

And all the time these quick flashes, images of bullets punching through my stomach, or my head. My grandpa used to have a book of photographs from *Life* magazine and there was this one from the Viet Nam war, a cop shooting a rebel through the head. The little revolver stuck up to his ear, his whole body wincing from it. About to die. I kept having this image, my skull smashing like a dropped dinner plate. Mom pulling a sheet back from my face at a morgue. I tried very hard not to think about these things, but the thoughts always came fluttering back, like insects around a porch light. Bumping and buzzing.

We turned up a lane and stopped in front of a perfectly circular gate in a massive white marble wall. Beyond the gate, I could just see a dim path heading into a gloomy forest of pine and cedar. The Ford settled in a cloud of dust, wheezing and pinging. I slipped the dolphin phone out of my purse, hit the speed dial for Emma's number and slid it under the front seat of the Ford, leaving it there like a live microphone. Hopefully it would record whatever happened next into her voicemail box.

A moment later, a young Asian woman walked through the gate, pacing toward us like a leopard. Wary. Restless. She was wearing a white silk jacket, baggy black pants, and sunglasses the color of wet asphalt. At her hip a cell phone and a folded-up fan with an ivory handle dangled from silver chains.

Me and the cops got out of the Crown Victoria. After the stink of the enclosed car, the air was fresh but cold. Bud stood with one hand on the driver side door, keeping the car body between himself and the leopard woman. A breeze ruffled the hem of her long jacket and flicked at her bangs. She looked

I'll be pushing up daisies soon.

at me with eyes as bleak as snow falling.

"Okay, Jun, so we're done, right?" Bud said, staring at the dusty road, littered with cedar needles. "Everyone knows we're out of it."

The leopard woman said, "You are finished. I promise you."

She turned back to me. "Come. Ancestor Lu is waiting."

*

Inside the gate, a dirt track disappeared into a dark wood. Giant evergreens towered around us, redwood and cypress and Douglas fir. They were staggeringly gigantic towers bursting from the earth, with roots as thick as sewer pipes. Lichens bulged out from them like pale tumors. The trees were unimaginably tall, and their dense canopy choked out the sun. Looking up, it was as if I had fallen to the bottom of a deep green well.

I had to hurry to keep up with Jun, trotting close enough to touch the ivory-handled fan swinging from her hip. Our muffled footfalls thumped like heartbeats as we tramped through the endless wood, and I had the sense, once again, of time opening up. My heart felt more and more quiet. My thoughts emptied out, until at last, though my limbs kept moving, it seemed as if we stood still, the leopard girl and I, while the wood like a deep brown river slid endlessly around us.

*

There was light ahead. I blinked and shook my head: waking up. The path was climbing steeply uphill. We had been walking in a deep ravine, and were now making our way up to the ridge. The trees were smaller and the light stronger. Jun climbed easily, lithe and restless. I scrambled after her, gasping and sweating and wishing I'd used more serious under-arm protection.

Jun topped the ridge and waited for me. I caught up and bent over with my hands on my knees, whooping for breath. Between gasps I saw a long sweep of bracken-covered hillside. The land was much rougher than it had looked from the windows of the Ford, especially upslope, where jagged humps and towers of bare rock thrust up like broken teeth from the hills.

From here the path was obvious again, a wide track beaten into the bracken. It climbed at an angle up to a huge stone gate, behind which rose the walls and upswept roof of a great manor. Its granite blocks and cedar beams erupted from the rugged slope as if the house were part of the rocky landscape, pushed from

118

the earth like the hills themselves. To the right, a silver waterfall plunged down a
towering granite face. Beside the falls, a few twisted pine trees grew out of cracks
in the slick rock.

Not far from the base of the falls, the water gathered into a deep pool. A
stream ran out from this pool and raced across the hillside. When we got to where
the path gathered itself into a little stone bridge, I squatted down at the water's
edge. The stream was fast but shallow here, racing here across a stony bed and
chattering with cold.

"Hey," Jun said sharply. "We do not keep Ancestor Lu waiting."

"We do if we smell like barf." So much of making a good first impression is
about confidence. No freaking way was I going to go into an interview with some
dude who might have me killed while I smelled like something left in a thermos for
a month. I scooped up a double handful of water to rinse out my mouth. The next
handful I drank. Then I splashed my face and slicked back my hair. "Okay," I said.

A young girl, maybe eight years old, came trotting downstream toward us.
Her arms were full of water lilies. "*Ni hao*, Jun!" She broke into a run. Her face
was half-black and half-Asian, her shirt and pants were soaking wet, and by the
time she reached us she was panting and grinning and dripping, hugely pleased
with herself. "Wah, Jun! You've brought someone from Outside!"

" *Ni hao*, Little Sister. I told you not to get wet again! You'll catch another
cold," Jun scolded.

"I was getting flowers for Papa!"

"No excuse! Run and tell Papa his guest is here."

"So I'm a guest, now," I said. "That sounds promising."

Little Sister tore up the hill, clutching her lilies. Jun watched her go. "Tell
me, Cathy … which do you like better: silk flowers, or real ones?"

How did she know my name? "Real, I guess."

"So does my father." Bitterness in Jun's voice. "He should think about that."

#

The gate to the manor was extraordinary—two marble pillars, carved into two
flowering peach trees with such skill that it seemed the next puff of wind might tear
the frail stone blossoms off and send them fluttering in the breeze. Resting at the
base of each tree was a white marble tiger. "Family likeness?" I asked, glancing at Jun.

If she thought that was funny, she hid it well.

Inside the gate, the courtyard was humming with business. Elegantly tailored young men wandered through the gardens talking on headset cell phones. Most of the talk was in Chinese, but whenever I heard a scrap of English, the conversation seemed to be about money.

Except for Little Sister, everyone was Chinese.

Jun's cell phone pinged, bumping against her thigh. She ignored it. "When he asks you a question, answer it. Don't try to lie, he can always tell. He'll probably want you killed anyway." She glared at me as if this was all my fault. "You don't have to make it inevitable. Watch your manners but don't cower. He doesn't care about cowering."

"Gee, thanks."

"Don't get the idea I like you," Jun said.

A gaggle of housemaids pointed at me and stared, chattering excitedly, until Jun's glare passed over them like a hawk's shadow, and they fell silent. "How humiliating," Jun muttered. "*This* house, reduced to sneaking around back alleys and killing little girls."

"Gosh, that *must* be embarrassing," I said. "Hey, I have a great idea. Why not let me go? I know you think this is wrong. Let me go, now, before something happens that we'll both regret."

"*To avoid shame, do nothing shameful.* My father may have forgotten this. I have not," Jun said bitterly. "I serve the house of Lu Tung Pin, in wisdom or folly. I won't betray him."

And my mom thought she got a lot of attitude from *me*. "This Ancestor Lu— he doesn't happen to fold paper birds, does he?"

Her thin lips tightened. "And ride a white donkey backwards?"

"The old man in the pawn shop!" I said. "Tsao's friend is Ancestor Lu?"

Jun bit off a long string of what I bet were words you couldn't say on Chinese network television. "Chang Kuo Lao—that meddling old sneak is not my father. I should have guessed we would find his stringy beard poking into this. *And* he has been talking to Tsao," Jun snarled. "Of course he has."

We turned into a doorway and entered what I took to be the family residence. Stone-flagged floors, covered here and there with simple rugs, and stone walls too, with thick cedar beams. Every few yards we passed stone lamps, carved in the shape of tigers, that hung from iron hooks. I imagined what it must be like to see them at night, when the oil-soaked wicks were lit—growls of white light through gleaming fangs.

Jun started down a passage toward the back of the residence, boots click-clacking on the stone floors. "He'll be in the Shrine Room." Unless I was completely turned around, we were headed straight into the mountain side. The passage seemed to grow narrower and darker, with fewer carpets on the floor and lamps hanging on the wall. I could feel the weight of rock pressing down.

We came to a gorgeous doorway, its two sides carved again into a pair of peach trees. Jun opened the door. Beyond it was a tall, dim stone chamber, something between a small cathedral and a giant mausoleum. As in a cathedral, there were niches cut into both walls. Some of these at the far end of the room were empty, but the near ones each held a jade cabinet and a small brazier. I counted nineteen of these, ten on the left and nine on the right, and all of the braziers were burning. Bright webs of fire flared and ebbed over the surface of the coals. The dim air was full of the crack and hiss of burning; pop and sigh, near and far, like half-heard voices. Ghosts talking, I thought. Dead voices. *I thought … and then he … I don't understand … I want to tell you, tell you, tell you….*

From the back of the chamber came a child's laugh. "Wait here," Jun said, tight-lipped. "He won't want to see us until he is finished talking to Little Sister."

I probably should have tried to run like hell as she walked forward. Instead, I inched over to the nearest shrine. Coals in the brazier smoldered and gleamed, throwing weak red light across the jade cabinet. After a lifetime of Saturday morning cartoons I guess I was expecting each shrine to be like a treasure chest: ancient coins and splendid swords and jewelry made from gold and jade. But while everything in the cabinet was obviously very old—unspeakably old—it was a strange collection of ordinary household things, the remnants of a life lived a thousand years ago. A dull bronze table knife, a stone jar with a cracked lid, a shallow dish stained with ink so old and dry it was flaking off, like ash. Three little bone buttons that might have come from a child's coat. A broken lute, fire-damaged on one side.

Jun's voice rose from the other end of the shrine room, spitting out sentences of angry Chinese.

I found a small jade box that rattled faintly when I gave it a gentle shake. I slid off the lid and tipped it towards the light so I could see inside. It was full of baby teeth. I snapped the lid back on, louder than I had meant to. The sound echoed through the dim chamber, and the voices across the room fell silent.

A moment later little footsteps came pattering out of the darkness at me, followed by the girl Jun had called Little Sister. She grinned. *"Ni hao!* Papa will see you now." She gave a little wave and darted through the doors back into the rest of the house.

122. Jun and her father were waiting for me in the furthest shrine on the left. The relics here were much more modern: a metal toy tractor, a tan army cap with a red star on the front, a little red book. A wad of bloody cotton. A spent shell casing and a flattened bullet. Jun was standing with her back to the cabinet, expressionless. Behind her, an old man—Ancestor Lu, I presumed—was holding a plastic picture frame, looking at a faded photograph of a plain Chinese girl standing on a factory floor. She had cheap shoes and drab overalls, accessorized with the sweetest, shyest smile. Slowly the old man put the picture back on the jade shelf, and turned around. He folded his hands and made a little bow. *"Ni hao,* Miss Vickers." His white beard was combed into three thrusting points. It was the old Chinese gentleman I'd met leaving the Eight Ancestors restaurant the day I went there to confront Victor.

"You!"

He smiled. "Me!"

So this was Ancestor Lu, who somehow had Bud and Perry on contract, or at least willing to do a little freelance kidnapping. I thought of the entry in Victor's day-timer—*7 pm New Chair.* "You're also the President of Intrepid," I breathed.

Jun said something in Chinese.

A look of concern crossed Lu's face as he patted his shirt pocket and brought out something like a small closed fan. "My daughter says you have been talking to Tsao. You haven't told him your birthday, have you, dear?" He flipped the fan open. Only it wasn't a fan. It was a knife.

"I'm not going to hurt you," he said. "Not yet, anyway." He stepped towards me. I stepped back. "Jun?"

7pm - New Chai

OK - actually P'eng L
Pharmaceuticals which bought Intrep
He must have gotten my license plate
from th
security d
here, bu
instead of giving it to the regular c
passed it on to Bud and Pe
I figure they got my address from the DMV and bugged Mom's

She held my wrists at my sides. She was very strong. I thought of kicking out at the brazier, but I didn't do it. Time slowed down. The old man reached toward me with the knife. Red light slid and winked like oil down the blade. I felt my pulse beating in my throat, slow as a funeral drum. Lu touched the edge of my jean jacket and gathered the lapel in his fingers. Fabric crinkled slowly, sliding against the skin of my neck. My heart was beating so hard it hurt my chest. "What are you doing?" I whispered.

He cut the top button off my jean jacket. "A memento," he said. "In case."

"In case what?"

He paused, tilting his head. "Tsao would like you. Jun, don't you think Tsao would like her?" He reached up for a lock of my hair and tugged it out straight. Time slowed down more. The knife drifted up before my eyes, and cut. I could feel my hair giving against the blade like thread tearing.

The old man stepped back. He dropped my button and the lock of hair in his shirt pocket, folded up his knife and put it away. Jun's hands relaxed around my wrists. My heartbeat sped up, hammering in my chest.

Jun turned her head sharply. "I think I hear something."

Red light made shadows pool and flicker around the old man's eyes. "I expect that will be Victor. My people saw him trailing the policemen who took you. He got in his car and followed you out here."

New pockets of terror kept flaring up inside me, like matches catching in my chest. "This isn't about me going to Intrepid at all. You're trying to trap Victor. I'm the bait."

Jun held up her hand, listening.

I held my breath. The coals on the brazier hissed and creaked. Finally I could hear it too—muffled shouts and crashes. Then a sharp firecracker bang.

Jun started to run back toward the door. "Wait," her father said. "The household knows what to do. They'll let him through."

Jun found a spot in the shadows behind the door. She drew a gun out from a holster under her armpit. In the middle of this madness, with my life very probably about to end, I found myself looking at her jacket and thinking *good tailoring*.

"If anyone's been hurt—" she started.

"—nothing is different," Lu said sharply. "Not in the long run. Not as things stand."

[handwritten notes:] So V's working on his Secret Project. Carla finds out, tries to play hardball with Lu. Bad move!!

The mausoleum door smashed open. Ancestor Lu put his hand over my mouth. Victor stood for an endless moment in silhouette. He was breathing hard, and there was a trickle of blood on his forehead. "Cathy?"

Time slowed down.

Jun stepped out from the shadows, two long strides, her legs like scissor-blades. The moment opened like a telescope. She raised her gun. I could hear the tiny click of the hammer going back. Then she shot him. A brass shell casing arced from the top of her gun, and a soot-stain the size of a baby's hand appeared on Victor's shirt. There was a hole in the middle of it.

Then came the noise, a deafening **blam** that rolled and boomed around the mausoleum. When the echoes finally faded, I could hear the last rattle and clink as the shell casing rolled to a stop on the stone floor.

Victor sagged back against the doorframe. Our eyes met. "I told you to stay out of this," he said. He sounded aggravated. He coughed. Blood leaked from the corner of his mouth.

Jun shot him again.

He staggered sideways and fell down in front of the first shrine, the one with the stone box of baby teeth. Red light from the brazier glimmered over his body.

*

Another shell casing jumped ringing out of Jun's gun, hot shiny brass. It reached the top of its arc and tumbled slowly to the floor. Clink, clatter, *ting*. Coals hissing and popping in the darkness around me. The smell of firecrackers bitter in my mouth.

*

The hem of Jun's jacket brushed the stone floor as she knelt beside Victor's body. She kept the gun in one hand. With the other she touched his neck, feeling for a pulse.

Victor's hand curled around the leg of the brazier. My heartbeat stopped.

Jun's eyes went wide. She tried to shoot him again.

Victor's body snapped like a coiling snake. Jun pulled the trigger of the automatic again and a stone chip flew out of the floor where Victor's side had been. Another gunshot crashed through the cavern. Victor smashed Jun in the side of the head with the brazier. Black lines and splotches appeared on her white jacket as red-hot coals spilled through the air.

Ancestor Lu let go of my hand.

My heart beat again.

Time sped up. Jun smashed onto the stone floor. Her gun went skittering away. Red-hot coals rained down like fireworks, breaking into ash and sparks as they hit the ground. The air stank of burning hair

Victor coughed and pulled himself onto his hands and knees. "Oh, my God," I breathed. "You're still alive. That's impossible."

The old man beside me stirred.

Jun lurched up to all fours. She looked around, spotted her gun lying on the floor and scrambled after it. Victor grabbed the red-hot grille from the toppled brazier, wrapping his fingers around it so the flesh on his hands popped and hissed like steak cooking. He dove after Jun and slammed the grille down on her hand as she reached for her gun. She jerked back, swearing, and her right hand curled up like a burnt spider. Her left snaked behind her back and brought out a butterfly knife. She flicked it open like a magician setting a dove free. In the red firelight, steel wings fluttered and danced.

Victor grabbed for the gun. He didn't make it. Jun kicked him in the head and he flew backwards, slamming into the jade shrine, knocking its ancient mementos out of their cubbies. A clay jar toppled over and smashed on the floor, spilling out its strange treasure: a long braid of soft black hair.

"Stop!" The old man beside me sprang forward. I hurried after him.

Victor grabbed the bronze knife that had fallen from the shrine and held it out unsteadily. Jun stood two paces away. Her butterfly knife made lazy looping circles in the dim air. "Father doesn't like it when you touch the family treasures," she said. "I'd put that down if I were you."

"I don't think I will." Victor glanced at his knife. It wasn't much of a weapon a dull bronze table knife that hadn't been sharpened for a thousand years. Victor's chest heaved with his ragged breath. "Cathy? You okay?"

"I'm not the one who got shot." I couldn't stop looking at the two neat bullet holes in the front of his shirt.

"Don't worry about him," Jun said. "He'll be fine. Won't you, Victor?"

Victor coughed, a horrible, gurgling cough, and then spat a mouthful of blood on the floor. "Shut up," he said. "I've got no problem hitting women. I'm a liberated guy."

"How contemporary," Jun said.

Victor leapt at her with his knife. He was fast, unbelievably fast. She was faster. A white blur; a flash of silver butterfly wings. Then they had changed places, and Victor had a long red line on each side of his face. "I've got no problems hitting men," Jun said.

Victor fingered his blood-slick cheek. "I see that."

Ancestor Lu knelt beside the broken jar of spilled black hair. Victor made a jump for him. The old man didn't even bother to look up as Jun kicked Victor, catching him square on the side of the face. He dropped like he'd been sand-bagged.

"I told you to leave my father's shrines alone," Jun said. "Dead people make him very sentimental. The living, not so much." Jun glanced over at me. "Hey, Cathy. Take a look at your boyfriend and tell me what you see."

The cuts on Victor's face had stopped bleeding. There were only fading char marks on the hand holding the bronze knife. He should have been crippled. Then again, after the gunshots, he should have been dead.

He should have been dead.

He should have been dead.

Figure/ground reversal: and suddenly, the world turned inside out.

Oh. My. God.

I might have said a word you can't say on TV, followed by, "Victor, when were you born?"

"Summer," he said. "Mid-July."

Jun laughed.

Everything I thought I knew was wrong. I felt sick. "What *year*, Victor?"

"I'm kind of busy right now," Victor said, still watching Jun. He glanced around, looking for a better weapon.

"You never get sick," I said. "You never get cold. You can fly a plane and work a microscope and you know World War One like you were there."

"You do have good eyes," Jun said. Behind her, Ancestor Lu righted the jade cabinet and carefully put back the pieces of his broken jar.

Victor lunged, slashing for Jun's eyes with the bronze knife. She dropped into a scything sweep-kick, spinning around one hand. Victor flew into the air like something spat from a lawn-mower. He smacked into the stone floor with a sickening crunch of snapping ribs.

Ten minutes ago, I would have been worried about him.

"Victor? When were you born?"

I thought of Giselle and little Bianca. Those '40s hairstyles. That wasn't a computer-retouched photo from a costume photography place. That picture had been taken on an Asian beach before Cambodia and Viet Nam had been invented—back when it was all French Indochina. "Tsao was only half-lying, wasn't he? You do abandon all your women. Not because you are going to die. Because you *aren't*."

"Tsao said *Victor* was going to die?" Jun barked with laughter. "Like him or hate him, Tsao does have wit."

And how about the money? The house, the plane, the paintings…. Victor had told me it all belonged to his uncle, but I had seen the property tax notice. Victor and the mysterious uncle were one and the same. Of course they were. No uncle bought a Chagall because his *nephew* was in love, and no young man had that much money.

But what about an old man who just *looked* young—a man old enough to have mining stock from the turn of the century. Old enough to have bought IBM and AT&T on the ground floor… "Victor," I said. "When were you born?"

"1885," he snapped. "There. Happy? 1885. End of the Comstock rush in Nevada. There. I said it. Now what?"

Ancestor Lu was studying the black hair lying pooled on the floor. Gently, he tried to reach under the soft braid, but at his touch it fell apart like ash. He cupped the black soot in his hands and placed it inside the broken jar. When he was done, his palms were black. He started to wipe them off on his pants, then stopped himself. When he finally looked back at Victor there was a terrible bleakness in his eyes, as if he had seen many massacres. As if he had ordered them. "That was precious to me," he said.

127.

*

Scattered about the floor, the coals from the overturned brazier were going out, one by one.

I had a sudden memory of my father. We must have been camping, because it was dark and we were sitting in front of a little fire by a lake. I was only half-listening as he talked, distracted by the pale bending colors of the fire. Flames licked black lines on the pale wood. *Without us, the world is just things, Cathy. It's our **seeing** that fills them with meaning. To pay attention is a painter's sacred duty. That's what real prayer is, real meditation: to hold your attention to the world like a match, until it catches with the fire of meaning.*

Sparks popped up, and the wind caught them, each brave flash a shooting star. A thin thread of light arcing through the darkness, and then blown out.

*

"Things pass. People die," Jun said tightly, staring at her father. "Even Little Sister will die. You know this. You have seen the blood tests. It is sad, yes, *but it is the way of things.*"

Lu said, "Then the way of things must change."

Victor feinted with the dagger. Jun's knife danced and Victor jerked back his hand, now laced in red. "Even you don't want to keep this up," she said.

"I've seen Victor's research," Lu said. "With the new science, there is hope."

"Science!" Victor spat out another mouthful of blood. "God, in all my life I've never done anything as boring as lab science. It's like watching paint dry— *really carefully.* As boring as being a soldier, and that's saying—" In the middle of his sentence he jumped at Jun again. She blocked him in a whirl of white jacket, and then she was stepping back, pulling the butterfly knife out of his kidney with a slick sucking sound. Victor screamed and dropped to his knees.

"I don't know. Being a soldier is pretty dull," Jun said. "When you take the fear of death out of it." She wiped her knife off on the back of Victor's shirt. "Tell Cathy what happened to Giselle. She's been jealous. It doesn't seem like one ought to be jealous of the dead," Jun said, "but it happens." Her face was expressionless.

"Giselle is dead," Victor said wearily. "Like all the rest of them. Killed in a car crash in 1948. Just a few months after that picture was taken."

"How convenient," Jun said.

I spun around. "*Shut up!*"

"No—she's right," Victor said. "That's the horrible part. I was devastated when the hospital called. Heartbroken. But even before I hung up the phone, I knew it was a godsend, too."

I stared at him.

"It bought me *time*, Cathy. Years and years with Bianca. For once it wouldn't have to be like it was with Penny, or Lucas, or Seung. I didn't have to leave. Bianca was so little. And kids, you know—they expect their parents to look the same forever."

"Wives are harder than children," Jun said. "Not so trusting."

The blood had already stopped running from Victor's slashed hand. "Couldn't last forever, of course, even with Bianca. I didn't keep any pictures in the house, I stayed away on business trips. But once a girl hits puberty, she starts thinking about bodies and what happens to them."

"Or doesn't," Jun said.

"I sent her to live with my sister. I had a good excuse," Victor said. "It was 1961 and everyone could see Indochina was going to hell."

"Frances?" I guessed. "Frances was your sister? And all those letters...?"

"You took those, too?" Victor stared at me. "You went back to my house and looked through my mail *again*?" I colored. "Did it ever occur to you that I might have a good reason for wanting to keep my life private?"

"It occurred to me. I just didn't care."

"Victor could have done worse," Jun said. "He could have decided to tell you his secret. Of course, he wouldn't be able to risk anyone else finding out—that would mean a life strapped to a table in a lab somewhere, donating tissue samples every day. If he told you, he'd have to take you somewhere safe, somewhere secret, and keep you there, and all your children, for as long as you lived," Jun said. "Then, cut off from the rest of your kind, you would get to watch as day by day your flesh sagged and year by year your bones grew brittle, while he never aged a day. You'd get ugly and lonely and desolate, but through it all he would tell you he loved you. As if that was any comfort."

Ancestor Lu regarded his daughter. "Now is not the time for this discussion."

"Now is exactly the time for it," Jun said.

Was it really possible that Victor had been born in 1885? He would have been twenty-one years old when the great earthquake hit San Francisco. Twenty-nine at the start of the First World War. Fifty-four when Hitler invaded Poland. Almost sixty when he met Giselle, fighting with the French resistance. Still looking twenty years old.

Victor looked at the old man. "What happens now?"

"You come work for me, as you should have done from the beginning." Lu shrugged. "The fight against death is my passion, Victor. That's why I founded P'eng-Lai. That's why I bought Intrepid, long before Carla showed me your work. You want to understand death." The old man touched the white prongs of his beard. "I want to end it."

"Golly, those are nice sentiments," I burst out. "What about Carla Beckman? How does shooting her in the stomach three times fit in with your mission statement?"

Ancestor Lu shrugged. "When she came to see me, it was obvious she had tissue samples from an immortal subject. She claimed the work was her own. Either she was immortal herself, or she had gained the confidence of one, or she was lying. I performed a test."

"A *test!*"

"You are forgetting the stakes. What risk would you take—even to your own soul, Miss Vickers—if you had a chance to save everyone?"

"But—"

"If you'd had a chance to save your father?"

The question took me like a bullet through the heart.

"Don't rush your answer," Jun said dryly. "In my experience, having a father has its ups and downs."

"Individual tragedies are regrettable, but not significant," Ancestor Lu said impatiently. "If the death of one person—or a thousand, or a hundred thousand—makes the end of Death itself more likely, only a fool would refrain from killing."

"Listen to my father," Jun said, her voice carefully neutral. "Those who have lived a long time see things differently than the rest of us. Don't you find it so, Victor?"

"God, I'm tired." Victor looked down at the bronze knife. "If I drop this, and come work with you, you have to promise nothing bad will happen to Cathy."

"I can make you rich," Lu said. "A patent that extended life by even a year would be worth billions."

"Who knows?" Jun said. "If you're really lucky, maybe you can delay death. Stop it, even. Surely that would be a great accomplishment," she said evenly. "Look how happy immortality has made you."

"Jun."

"And how kind," she continued. "What a solace it must be, knowing that, whatever happens, it can all happen again tomorrow. So comforting," she said blandly. "Some might worry that the lives of ordinary people would come to seem cheap to an immortal. The world's an ant farm after a century of two, right? Millions struggle and perish, more millions take their place." She shrugged. "Some might think that a man who was bitter, or jealous, or disappointed, but knew he could take a punch or a bullet with impunity—some might worry that such a man might do terrible things." She gave Victor a long, level look. "But that would be taking such a dark view of human nature, don't you think?"

Victor was pale. "What do you know?"

"People," she answered.

The mausoleum door pushed open. Little Sister peeked through the crack, looking scared but determined. "Papa?"

"Wah!" Lu said. He spoke to her softly in Chinese.

"I won't go." Little Sister glared at Victor. "You get out of here!"

"Or what?"

Little Sister gave a grunt and lifted up an automatic so the barrel showed in the crack of the door.

Victor's eyebrows rose. Ancestor Lu suppressed a smile.

"That's my gun!" Jun said.

"You weren't using it." Little Sister shrugged. "It's not my fault you didn't lock the safe."

Ancestor Lu walked quickly forward, ignoring Victor and his knife. He knelt in front of the door. "This is not a toy. You could get hurt."

At that instant I happened to look up at Jun. Her expressionless mask had slipped, and there was something like anguish on her face as her father gently took the gun from the little girl's hand.

Things pass. People die. Even Little Sister will die. You know this. You've seen the blood tests.

I looked at the old man as he folded Little Sister's small dark hands inside his own. "You aren't in it for the money at all," I said. "You want Victor to think that, but this is all about her, isn't it?"

"I'm not quite that sentimental," Lu said, still holding Little Sister's hands.

But Jun was looking at me with fear and wonder, as if some terrible idea was written on my forehead. "Good eyes," she whispered.

Watching her face in the long, loaded moment that followed was like seeing a candle go out, or watching a stream freeze over. A cold stiffness spread out from her eyes like frost until her face was once again expressionless. Jun stepped toward the door. As the butterfly danced in her hand, I realized she meant to kill Little Sister.

"Not the girl!" I yelled. Sparks scattered around my feet as I threw myself forward. Steel flashed as I slammed into the door, knocking Little Sister back into the corridor. I fell awkwardly and put my hand on a coal and jerked it off again. There was a thump and then a crash as Victor tackled Jun. In the hallway outside the Shrine Room, Little Sister was crying. Probably just bruised and startled by getting slammed with the door, I thought. Probably she didn't even realize Jun had just tried to cut her throat.

I hoped not.

Jun thought her father's fight against death was an old man's fatal folly, driven not by principles, but by his love for Little Sister. The bleak understanding I had seen form in her eyes was that the only way to stop Lu's mad quest was to kill the girl.

Victor and Jun rolled over the dying coals, gasping and fighting.

"*Stop!*" Lu said. The struggle went suddenly quiet.

I was curled in a heap at the bottom of the mausoleum door. My hand hurt, and my shoulder, and I thought I might have twisted my ankle. Jun's knife was buried in the wooden doorframe, right next to my eye. There was a stinging line of fire along my cheek, and something wet and salty trickled past my mouth. When I touched my fingertips to my face, they came up red.

Jun was on her back on the floor. Victor was on top of her. He had one hand wrapped in her long hair, and the other held the bronze dagger to her throat. She offered no resistance—just lay there, impassive, her face as stiff as a mask.

Lu called out in Chinese. Little Sister wailed an answer from the hallway.

"Get up," the old man told Victor.

"I don't think—"

"Get. Up."

Victor got up.

Ancestor Lu said something to Jun in Chinese. She crawled to her feet and stood before him. He looked at her for a long, grim moment.

Jun said, "Do you think you would love her so much if she was forever?"

"Go," he said. "You are not my daughter." He took the bronze dagger from Victor and put it in its place, turning his rigid back on Jun. She looked at him. Then she opened the door, stepped over the sobbing child in the corridor, and walked away.

Feb 8 Late Night
(Hour of Omigod Carpal Tunnel Syndrome from Typing All Day)

"Now what?" Victor said again.

"You stay with me," Lu said.

"To be strapped to a table all day? Tissue samples. Blood tests. Bits of my liver torn out and regrown?"

"If that is what is necessary." No sign of sympathy in the old man's eyes. No sign he cared at all.

"What about Cathy?"

"She'll be safe."

"Safe at home?" I said. "Safe as in I get to walk around in the world and don't have to worry about waking up at the bottom of the ocean with some bullet holes in my stomach?"

"Not at home," the old man said, surprised. "You can never go home." He glanced around the mausoleum. "This is your home now."

Victor's fingers flexed around the knife. "I can't accept that," he said.

"You are here, in my house. Many men with guns stand between you and the free air. If you try to leave, they will shoot Cathy. I gave the orders hours ago.

You can agree to work with me, and have the girl by your side, or you can struggle and see her die and work for me all the same. Those are your only choices," said Ancestor Lu.

I imagined Mom waiting by the phone for me to call. Face gone gray. Waiting and waiting.

Victor looked at me. "If you have any good ideas for a miracle rescue, now would be the time."

Before I could speak, the door banged open and Little Sister ran in, wild-eyed. "Papa! The police are here—dozens and dozens of them! They came in helicopters—I saw them arresting Wei Po and his men!"

Victor stared at me. "Good job," he said at last.

*

Ten minutes later I was standing in Ancestor Lu's courtyard, just inside the gate with the carved peach blossoms over it. Blue-uniformed policemen were escorting Ancestor Lu's people into an ever-increasing number of police vehicles. No sign of Jun, though—she must have escaped before they showed up. A paramedic was putting a bandage on Victor's hand. I was talking to a detective. You could tell he was in charge because he didn't have to wear a uniform or anything.

"We tracked you by your cell phone," he explained. "When a cell phone is on, it sends a little ping out to the nearest transmission towers so the network can find it for incoming calls. If we know the cell number, we can get the phone company to track the pings and use triangulation to find the exact location of the phone." He hesitated. "To be honest, the officer who took the 911 call didn't know that. Your friend explained it to him and begged him to tell me."

"My friend?" I said, breaking into a grin. "My friend Emma, that would be?"

The cop nodded. "She sure does know a lot about phones."

I couldn't keep from laughing.

Two cops came up with Victor between them. "What about this one, sir?"

"He's one of the good guys," I said, giddy with the wonderful feeling that I wasn't actually going to be shot to death or imprisoned here for the rest of my life. I fluttered my eyes at Victor. "He came to save me, officer. He L-O-V-E's me."

"I'll bet he does," the cop said dryly. "But he's got powder burns on his shirt

134.

and knife marks all over his clothes and I think we'll ask him to go downtown, thank you very much."

"Is that necessary?" Victor said tightly. My smile faded at the tone of his voice. He wasn't liking this at all.

"I'm afraid so," the policeman said. "Shouldn't be a big deal for one of the good guys, right?"

Victor shrugged, but I could tell his nonchalance was an act.

I thought of the bullet holes in his chest. They'd be giving a closer look at those, wouldn't they? What would a doctor make of bullet holes that healed themselves? What would happen in three hours if they unwrapped that bandage and found Victor's hand clean and unmarked underneath it? For a hundred and twenty years Victor had been hiding who he was. What he was. For all I knew, he had killed to protect that secret. The arrival of the police meant freedom for me: but if he wasn't lucky, Victor's life might be headed for the same nightmare— strapped to a table in a lab somewhere, a guinea pig for military scientists.

[handwritten margin notes: logical cost / reproduction. / Like bats / Long life / = / fewer kids...]

"Officer, could I have just a moment with Cathy before we go?"

"Sure. I won't stop a handsome prince from collecting his kiss," the cop said with a smile. He turned to supervise his men, and Victor and I drifted over a few steps, so we were right beside the gate, talking quietly together under a spray of carved peach blossoms. "So now you know," he said.

"Yeah." I wanted to take his hand, but I didn't. "You can't let them find out, can you?" Victor shook his head. "How are you going to do it? Escape? You won't have to...you aren't going to kill any cops, are you?"

A brief dry smile. "I'll try lawyers first."

"I guess you can afford a good lawyer."

"*Lots* of good lawyers."

Through the gate, like a landscape in a picture frame, the coastal range spread out before us. Further away, the ocean, a hazy blue blur at the horizon. "How old is Bianca now?"

"Fifty-seven. It was her birthday the day we met," Victor said. "11/11. Remembrance Day."

I thought back to that first meeting on the seawall, me there with my sketchpad out, the cormorant like a messenger. Fate about to step in.

135.

Victor said, "I have my good decades and my bad ones. The 80s were bad.
I woke up in a hotel room in Bangkok one day and there was a story on CNN—
Scientists Winning War Against AIDS. AIDS was a big deal in Thailand—sex trade,
you know. And I thought, maybe I could learn about *me*." He laughed. "I had this
comic book idea about science—the lone genius in the lab. Nobody ever told me
there was all this *reading* you had to do. All these *meetings*." He shrugged. "I've
learned some things. It's a recessive gene, immortality is. Hard to pass on. God,
how I watched my own kids, the first few years. I nearly poked Lucas with a pin to
see how fast he'd heal."

"Tell me about the needle mark in my arm."

"I was working on a blood test. I wanted to be able to tell if someone else was
immortal, or at least carrying the trait. I sort of volunteered you to be my first test
subject."

"Why?"

"You just really want to make me say this out loud, don't you?"

I looked at him, mystified.

"Because I was hoping to spend my life with you, dummy!"

"Oh," I said.

Victor coughed and spat out a stream of saliva and blood.

"I know you've just been shot twice through the lungs and all, but horking up
gobs of blood is sort of dragging down a romantic moment here, V."

"I wanted you to test positive so bad, Cathy. My hand was shaking so hard I nearly
dropped the test tube when I did the assay." He looked down at the silver pocket
watch still dangling from his belt. "It's a hundred year fantasy, you know—not to be
alone, for once. To find someone who wouldn't… leave, the way you all leave."

Leave as in *die*. I shivered. "Don't suppose I passed the test, by any chance?"

"No," he said.

Bummer. But not surprising. I guess that was another hidden lesson of the
time I jumped off the garage roof and broke my ankle: you are not immortal. In
the real world, nobody can fly. In the real world, nobody lives forever.

Almost nobody.

"I may not be immortal, but I'm here," I said. "You're not alone."

"Not for lack of trying." He spat again. "I have worked *so hard* not to love you."

136.

"Don't be hard on yourself. I'm very loveable."

"Yeah," he said. "I noticed." He reached out and let his fingers trace the cut Jun had left on my cheek, and my face went hot.

"You know," I said, "my Mom isn't in the next room, for once."

"I guess not."

I brushed his bangs away from his eyes. "And Emma isn't lurking inside one of these damn cop cars waiting to pop out, right?"

"I wouldn't think so."

I slid my hands down to his neck, cupping his face. "And I left my cell phone in Bud and Perry's car," I whispered. He looked at me with hungry eyes. I tilted his mouth down to mine. "I think I'm going to kiss you," I said.

And I did.

*

"Wow," he said breathlessly, some long time later.

"What?"

"It was like time stopped."

I smiled. "That happens sometimes."

Feb 9, afternoon
(Happy Birthday to Me)

Sunday afternoon. No word from Victor yet, but nothing on the 10 O'Clock News, either, so I guess the lawyers are doing their thing.

Spent all yesterday writing down what happened. At least I'll have something to show the police psychiatrist when the guys in the white coats take me away.

Mom's clattering around in the kitchen. She traded off-days so she could be home for my 18th birthday. She's in there right now making cake. Dad always used to do something weird with food coloring. Last year it was a bright blue angel-food cake, with lemon-flavored icing the color of blood.

—> Doorbell just rang. Bounced up, thinking it was Victor, but I can hear Emma and her Dad in the hallway. I had something philosophical and profound to say, but now I'm wondering if they brought any really cool presents, so I might as well go be Festive...

(handwritten marginalia:) 137.

Birthday Menu

chicken baked
Sherry
honey-ginger
Carrots
mashed potatoes
with gravy

Greek Salad

No washing up !!!

Go Mom!

Feb 9, afternoon
(Happy Birthday to Me, Happy Birthday to Me!)

"I liked it better when saving your life meant helping you with algebra," Emma growled as she came through the door, but she grabbed me and hugged me hard.

"Thanks," I said hoarsely. I had to break the hug early so I wouldn't start crying and ruin my mascara.

"Pretty peonies for birthday girl!" Mr. Cheung said, beaming and handing me a bouquet of beautiful silk flowers. "Peony my favorite flower," Mr. Cheung said. "Very good luck. After New Year, whole family used to go to flower market and buy this, still in bud. If they open, that mean good luck and prosperity for the next year. I once worked for a flower-seller—terrible time! If any flowers not open, *Wah!* Angry people!" He smiled. "This one open, OK!"

"No problem there," I said slowly, fingering the blossoms. "It's a sure thing, isn't it?"

Tell me, Cathy … which do you like better: silk flowers, or real ones?

I guess if Ancestor Lu is successful, we'll all be silk flowers, won't we?

#

A couple of times during my birthday dinner Emma tried to talk to me in private, keeping her voice low and starting to explain some research she had been doing. Before she could get anywhere, though, her Dad burst in, grinning. "Whisper whisper—all talk about boys, yes! Tsk Tsk! Maybe you help her out, Cathy. Find a bee for my pretty flower?" he teased.

"Dad!"

After a couple of glasses of wine, Mom and Emma's Dad got positively jolly. Mr. Cheung started telling stories about his youth. "Very poor!" he said, waggling one finger around the table at us. "No money! Every day chicken feet! One day, I say to my mother, If we eat chicken feet, *who eat chicken?* That very day, I decided when I grow up—"

"**I will eat chicken!**" Emma chorused with him, rolling her eyes.

"Young people don't know." Mr. Cheung smiled at my Mom, who was pouring us cups of decaf. "They have all this money, but worry also! Emma, other day, find first gray hair!"

"*Dad!*"

"Seventeen year old!" He tsked. "Too much worry."

"*DAD!*"

"She tell many Cathy story, but I still think your daughter good girl." He nodded reassuringly to Mom. "Except for time start car on fire," he admitted. "Then… little worry."

Mom put the coffee back in the kitchen and returned carrying a tray on which sat a hot-pink pie topped with eighteen wobbling candles.

"*Happy Birthday to you…*

Happy Birthday to you!"

The doorbell ding-donged—Victor! I jumped up and ran to the hallway as I belted out,

"*Happy BIRTH-DAY dear Me-EEEEEEEEEE!*"

I pulled on the door and threw my arms open and jumped so Victor and me could do that thing like on TV where the boy grabs the girl and spins her around in the air.

Only the man standing there wasn't Victor. It was Tsao.

Happy Birthday… toooooooooo … YOUOOUOUOUOUOUOU!

"Grk," I said, as I unwrapped my arms and slid awkwardly down Tsao's front. So much for never telling him how old I was, or when my birthday fell.

"I was looking for Victor," he said politely. "I expected to find him here."

"Me too," I said.

"Nice to see you again, Mr. Tsao," my mother said. "Come in and have some pie." She pulled out a chair for him. Tsao settled next to me.

"Miss Vickers," he said, "you were born on the first day of the year of the Fire Tiger. I should have known."

I shot a glance over at Emma, wondering what the heck that meant, but she just shrugged.

Mom put the hot pink concoction in front of me. Judging by the smell, and the electric orange Nilla wafers on top, I guessed it was a banana cream pie. "Happy birthday," Tsao said.

Time got sticky as I took a deep breath. Air slowly filled my lungs. The

TYGER, TYGER

139

dancing candle flames grew old before my eyes: slowing, faltering, and finally still, as if each were the soul of a life that had run its course.

I felt Tsao's eyes on me as I started to blow. The frightened candles shivered and went out.

*

Then Tsao and the others were clapping and time was running right again.

I cut slices of pie.

"So nice you have us!" Mr. Cheung said, digging in. "Mm! Delicious! Emma, you try! Emma all the time worry."

Emma poked gingerly at a bright green banana slice.

"It's perfectly safe," my mom told her, straight-faced. "I kept it overnight in the organ freezer at work to make sure it wouldn't go bad."

"My daughter have idea for business," Mr. Cheung explained, "but we have small-time cash-flow issue. She worry we won't find investor." He chuckled at the absurdity of the idea. "All it takes for business is one good idea, and a people of high net worth."

"Yeah—I need my own personal George Wingfield," Emma said, giving me a Meaningful Look. Wingfield…Oh, right. The guy who had given Victor his investment advice.

"Is he that Australian that owns FOX?" Mom asked. She handed me a wine glass full of sherry. "Happy eighteenth honey. Why don't you make a toast?"

"No, Wingfield made it big about a hundred years ago," Emma said. "He's the guy who decided to base Nevada's economy on the Big Three: mines, casinos, and divorce. He died in 1959." She gave me another Meaningful Look and raised a forkful of pie to her mouth.

"Our business no problem," Mr. Cheung said. "Yesterday, I get big Hell money, one million dollars, and I make offer to Chung Li Ch'uan and Ancestor Lu."

The wine glass dropped from my numb fingers, smashing spectacularly on our floor and spattering sherry over everybody's pant-legs. "Who?" I asked thickly through a mouthful of pie.

Mom jumped up and ran for some paper towels. "Everybody stay still while I get the glass up."

"What did you say?" Emma asked, staring at her dad. "Who is Ancestor Lu?"

"Wah! My American daughter does not even know the Eight Immortals!" Emma's dad shook his head. "Very great, very powerful. Travel all over China. Chung Li Ch'uan is CEO, most old, very prosperous. Ancestor Lu, he is always travel around world, looking to help good people. They say to very best he make immortal, too!"

"A dangerous gift," Tsao remarked. He glanced at me. "The world is full of pain, and an endless life is endless pain. Either that, or you have to stop caring. Mortality is the human condition, I think. To lose death is also to lose what is precious in life." He looked at the silk flower beside my place.

Tsao has been talking to Jun, I thought. He knows her and her father Ancestor Lu. Ancestor Lu is immortal. I bet Jun is too, I thought, my mind still racing. That's why she was willing to kill Little Sister. Dead at 10, or 35, or 90, it wouldn't make that much difference, would it? The bullet had been fired at Little Sister's heart the day she was born mortal, Jun must have thought. Exactly when it hit wouldn't make much difference.

Mom crouched next to the table. "Hey, birthday girl. I suppose you don't have to help clean up, but you could at least lift your feet."

"God, I'm sorry. I just—" *I just realized my boyfriend isn't the only immortal.* Okay, that's an excuse the average mom will buy, no problem. I scrambled out of my chair and helped clean up.

"When I was a boy," Mr. Cheung said, "we sell all the time flower for offering Eight Immortals at the flower market. Chung Li Ch'uan and Ancestor Lu, Ho Hsien Ku the housewife, and Lan Ts'ai Ho (who looks after flower-sellers!) Han Hsiang Tzu, the musician, Iron Crutch Li, Chang Kuo Lao riding backwards on his donkey…" He scratched his head, and started counting on his fingers.

"I think you've missed Tsao Kuo Chiu," Tsao said blandly.

I started up in shock, and smacked my head on the table so hard it made the forks rattle. Tsao bent over to peer at me, amused. "He was always my favorite. An immortal with nice clothes and a good sense of humor."

"Right! Yes!" Emma's Dad beamed. "The Sung prince who murdered the husband of a beautiful woman because he wanted her for his own."

Tsao's expression went still. "The brother did the killing."

"Could be," Mr. Cheung said agreeably. "Much long time ago. Million dollar hell money, though, Chung Li Ch'uan and Ancestor Lu, I think they notice that. You mark my word, in no time we see person of High Net Worth come do deal with Emma. Immortals take care of good peoples."

Tsao glanced back and forth between Emma and me, with laughter in his eyes. "As a matter of fact," he said, "I might have a little money to invest."

Feb 9, Evening
(First Hour of the Rest of My Life)

A fedex guy came to the house with a letter for me just as the party was breaking up. Tsao had left, Mom was tidying in the kitchen. "Emma! Time to go!" Mr. Cheung said, getting into Emma's car. Now that he's living with her, he wants to do all the driving even though he doesn't have an American license.

"I'll be there in a minute!" she called from the porch as I opened the Fedex.

It was from Victor. A short note, written fast. Handwriting shaky, as if he were doing it while riding in a car, or a plane.

Cathy—

Ancestor Lu has disappeared. I have to find him and find out what he is doing. I'll come back when I can. It might be a while before you hear from me again. Maybe even a year or two. I've been waiting so very long for you; I guess I can wait a little longer. At least your Mom will be pleased—the next time we meet, we'll be the right age for each other!

Take care of yourself, and keep your eyes open. Watch for signs of Ancestor Lu, but don't be scared. You have more friends than you know—powerful ones, looking out for you. I can't tell you much, but I can tell you we didn't meet by accident.

Remember the dress you wore when we went out, and crème brûlée dripping down my face. Remember the cormorant on the rock the day we met, and late nights talking. Remember that I came for you in the shrine room at Ancestor Lu's place and I will come for you always. Remember sitting on tirehenge, drinking root beer. Forget the names because names lie but remember us because when you look at me I remember myself.

Remember me because I will never forget you.

V.

*

142.

I looked up at Emma. "Don't!" she said, wiping my cheeks with her hand. "You'll drip on your letter."

I nodded, sniffling, and folded up Victor's note.

Mr. Cheung honked his horn. "My dad has a great new business idea. Selling Amway products, god help us," Emma said. "I set up a meeting with your friend Tsao, though. He wants to invest in DoubleTalk."

I tried to smile. "The 30/30 plan is still a go."

Emma looked at me, hands on hips. "Are you going to be okay?"

"Ancestor Lu escaped."

"Of *course* he did."

"Cathy?" Mom called from inside. "Is everybody gone?"

"Almost," I said. "Emma, Victor's going away too. I think there's a war coming—a war of the immortals."

The world seemed big and strange to me. How could anything be the same any more? You put a quarter in the cap of a guy panhandling at the BART station and wonder if he was alive to see Rome fall. Emma told me once that baking powder was an act of love, invented by a chemist for his wife, who was allergic to yeast. Now here was Ancestor Lu, trying to end death itself for the sake of a mortal wife and an eight year-old girl.

My father would have done the same for me.

"Hey—no crying," Emma said. "You've got a driver's license and you can vote. You're wearing your favorite silk shirt and your coolest leather jacket, right?"

I made a sad little hiccupping laugh. "A killer coat of Lipslicks in "Daring", and strictly smear-proof mascara," I said, wiping my eyes.

"The cops will be coming back to talk to you," Emma said. "With Lu and Victor gone."

"Oh, jeez. You're right. What am I going to tell them?"

"Tell them everything," she said. "Print out your diary and give them the letters and make them dial all the phone numbers and show them your sketches, because you know what?" she said, with her special little Emma smile. "They won't believe a word of it."